PRAISE FOR *TALE*

This is the first comprehensive discussion on talent intelligence that I have seen. This is a topic much discussed but little understood. Toby has finally given us a clear definition and a practical way to implement this powerful process.
Kevin Wheeler, founder of the Future of Talent Institute

Toby Culshaw has written an insightful book to help you execute your talent strategy. What I like most about *Talent Intelligence* is how actionable it is. Toby shares years of his learnings and experience, and he explains in detail how you can apply it yourself through practical steps.
Anita Lettink, keynote speaker and adviser on the future of work, partner at Strategic Management Centre and founder of HRTechRadar

Wow, from the maestro of TI – Toby himself. I was honoured when asked to read the book and comment. It is jam-packed with practical advice and real examples of talent intelligence in all its forms: a must-read for business leaders and HR leaders alike who want to drive smarter business decisions. To quote from the text, 'the shifting mindset of operational to strategic is critical'. Loved all of it – I will be buying the book for every member of our team for sure.
Alison Ettridge, founder of Stratigens

It's all about the data and the insights we can draw from it. I've felt this for a long time. This book and the work Toby has done confirms to me that this is a game changer! In an ever-changing and highly competitive world the notion and discipline of talent intelligence is, for me, an essential part of an integrated talent strategy – not only to compete but to win.
Denise Haylor, former CHRO of Royal Philips and Flextronics, and Managing Director and Partner of Boston Consulting Group

Toby is a recognized and trusted expert in talent intelligence – over the years he's proved to be one of the key leaders in this developing field. It's exciting to see how TI is developing and becoming more recognized as a valuable source of meaningful and actionable insights business leaders can leverage. In this text he brings together these experiences and a wide range of sources; it's a thorough essay on TI space and key reading for anyone interested in developing this knowledge.
Giles Harden, SVP People at INFARM

Toby Culshaw and his insight on the function of Talent Intelligence takes on and excels at creating a lexicon and foundational set of practices in the young and ever-growing space of Talent Intelligence. Creating a process is plenty hard, as is scoping a business case for change – both of which are in this text – yet defining a language for others to use in years to come is even harder. I am looking forward to applying many of these principles and labels to the products and services I use for the public and private sector companies we serve. Other leaders in recruiting, workforce planning and analytics should review this lexicon and render it into their own work.
Andrew Gadonmski, Managing Director of Aspen Analytics

The most inclusive and comprehensive work on Talent Intelligence I've seen to date. Toby captures the art and science of this continually evolving craft and the emerging technology platforms, complete with concrete and impactful examples. A must-read for all leaders who see their competitive advantage coming from deeply understanding and acting on distilled insights from the internal and external talent landscape.
Cortney Erin, Vice President, Global Talent Acquisition at Microsoft

A timely and comprehensive examination of an often under-explored but critical area of talent strategy. Toby manages to come up with something for everyone – from early to late adopters – as well as write a bit of a love letter to the subject.
Teresa Wykes, Global Head, Talent Intelligence at SAP

Talent Intelligence

Use business and people data to drive organizational performance

Toby Culshaw

KoganPage

First published in Great Britain and the United States in 2022 by Kogan Page Limited

2nd Floor, 45 Gee Street	8 W 38th Street, Suite 902	4737/23 Ansari Road
London	New York, NY 10018	Daryaganj
EC1V 3RS	USA	New Delhi 110002
United Kingdom		India
www.koganpage.com		

Kogan Page books are printed on paper from sustainable forests.

ISBNs
Hardback   978 1 3986 0725 5
Paperback   978 1 3986 0723 1
Ebook   978 1 3986 0724 8

British Library Cataloguing-in-Publication Data
A CIP record for this book is available from the British Library.

Library of Congress Cataloging-in-Publication Data
2022031462

Typeset by Hong Kong FIVE Workshop
Print production managed by Jellyfish
Printed and bound by CPI Group (UK) Ltd, Croydon CR0 4YY

Dedicated to my father.
You were my biggest cheerleader – kind, generous, funny, smart,
compassionate, brave and an eternal optimist.
You were the father we all can only wish for and hope to emulate.
You were larger than life and loved and were loved in equal measure.
You are missed and there will always be a hole in our lives
where you once stood. I think of you always and have had more than
a few conversations with you in my head about this book while writing it.
I like to think you would have been proud.
Thank you for everything.

Without data, you're just another person with an opinion.
W Edwards Deming

CONTENTS

LIST OF FIGURES

ABOUT THE AUTHOR

Toby Culshaw is currently Talent Intelligence Leader, Consumer Operations, at Amazon. Amazon is an American multinational technology company employing over a million workers, globally focusing on e-commerce, cloud computing, digital streaming and artificial intelligence. In his role at Amazon, he is deeply immersed in developing the field of talent intelligence, supporting key company executives on crucial decisions with a global impact and developing out a Talent Intelligence Consulting and Advisory capability.

He assumed this role after leaving Royal Philips in October 2020 where he was the Global Head of Talent Intelligence. Royal Philips is a Dutch multinational health technology organization that currently employs around 80,000 people across 100 countries. Within Philips he built their talent intelligence function out from just himself to a globally dispersed, award-winning and industry-recognized benchmark team, impacting hundreds of decisions and billions of dollars' worth of investment and spend across the organization.

Toby is also the founder of The Talent Intelligence Collective – a global community that endeavours to develop, support and inspire its members as well as promote ethical integrity and best practice in all aspects of Talent Intelligence, Talent Research, Labour Intelligence, Human Capital Intelligence, Competitor Intelligence and more.

He is an international speaker on talent strategy, people analytics, talent intelligence and the workforce of the future. He has been recognized as one of the 11 most influential in-house recruiters by *Recruiter* magazine for a record fourth time – consecutively in 2017, 2019, 2020 and 2021.

Toby has 15 years' experience working in a number of guises: external search, internal recruitment, internal executive recruitment and RPO, and he ran his own research firm. The key for Toby throughout has been using the data, insight and intelligence gathered through research/search activities to have a true business impact.

FOREWORD
Talent Intelligence has arrived

Talent Intelligence has emerged as one of the most important new disciplines in business. Why? Quite simply, we can now use data and analytics to understand the labour market, our workforce and our organization like never before.

Historically, companies operated in functional silos. The recruiting team set out to find candidates and source positions. The training department tried to identify skills gaps and new capabilities to build. The people analytics team did surveys to find reasons for high turnover or labour strife. And the workforce planning team worked with finance to put together headcount plans and organization structures.

Today this model no longer works. Companies in every industry are transforming their businesses into new business models, new businesses and adjacent industries. Oil companies are getting into solar and hydrogen. Telecommunications companies are moving into digital services, payments and consulting. Banks are getting into cryptocurrency and cyber operations. And retailers are moving into healthcare, delivery and omni-channel distribution.

In every one of these cases, the CEO and CHRO has to hire, staff and organize a new team of people with new skills, new pay structures and possibly new careers. Can the traditional model work? The answer is no.

Our research, which we've been doing over the last two years, shows that the real solution to growth is an integrated combination of what we call the Four R's: Recruiting, Retention, Reskilling and Redesign. Companies need to look at location, skills and source of hire, as well as the organization structure, pay model and even work arrangements, in a holistic way. Who can help make these decisions? The Talent Intelligence team.

Talent Intelligence is the new domain where sourcing analytics, skills analytics, workforce planning and people analytics merge. It is a role where labour economists and workforce planning come together. And it's a group and staff team that can help with organization design, skills development and recruiting.

I want to applaud Toby for taking the time to write this book and help us all understand the role of Talent Intelligence going forward. This is an important and strategic new domain, and one which I believe brings data and AI to business in some of the most strategic ways ever seen.

Josh Bersin, Global Industry Analyst (www.joshbersin.com)

ACKNOWLEDGEMENTS

It would be remiss of me not to say a few, or not so few, words of thanks to some of the amazing people who have contributed, supported, encouraged and frankly survived the process of me writing this.

First, my family. I'm so sorry for how often I've talked about this book. Natalie, you are my rock. You may not work in Talent Intelligence but I fear you could write a book on it now given how often I've spoken to you about it. Thank you for all you do and all you are. You are more than I could ask for and the support that allows me to do what I do. Boys, if you ever read this, thank you for everything – all those early mornings, all those interruptions to talk about Roblox, for being out the window playing in the garden on your swings for me to look at for inspiration as I have written this book. You all give me the drive, energy and courage to take on anything; you bring me joy each and every day. Thank you from the bottom of my heart for all you are.

To my brother and sisters, thank you for all your support. If you've made it to this point you will finally know what I do for a living. I hope it was as exciting for you to learn about it as it has been for me to write about it.

Mum, this has been the toughest 18 months of our lives and you have been a rock throughout. Your continued drive and energy have been inspirational. Throughout my career, along with Dad, you've always been my biggest supporter and cheerleader even when you had no idea what I did for a living. I wouldn't be where I am today, or the man I am today, without you. Thank you for all your passion, your unconditional love, your continual sacrifices for us all. You are inspirational.

You are all my world. I love you more than anything, thank you.

To those in the Talent Intelligence community and the Talent Intelligence Collective, a huge thank you to you all for all your honest, open and enlightening conversations and support. Every day I am enthused about the potential of this function/industry. Never before have vendors had such a close and transparent relationship with their customers and potential customers. They are all so supportive, so enthusiastic. We really wouldn't be the same without you. To couple that with practitioners who are so open for sharing best practice, so transparent about the problems they're facing, their troubles, their successes, their challenges. To name but a few: Alison Ettridge,

Nick Brooks and Alan Walker. You get a special shout-out for being my partners in crime for the Talent Intelligence Collective Podcast and everything that comes along with it, but of course none of that would happen without the amazing Ellen Laird and Sarah Clayton. How you two deal with us all I've no idea – it's like herding cats on catnip. You are brilliant. Thank you to you all.

Jay Tarimala, thank you so much for all your contributions, both to this book and also the community as a whole. Your passion for sourcing and intelligence is infectious. Don't ever stop having that drive and energy; you are a force of nature. Thank you for all your support. Lyndon Llanes, Teresa Wykes, Kim Bryan, James Brown, Jacob Madsen, Jose Garcia, Barry Hurd, Arnab Mandal, Daorbhla Smyth, Kaylee Baldassin, Lee Yi Ting, Molly Starkey, Kim Haemmerle, Evdokia Pappa, Rachel Engrissei, Sean Armstrong, Prashanth Kalyani, Soumalya Pyne, Kaylee Baldassin, Jennifer De Maria, Jenni Lenz, Aliza Goldstein, Rishi Banerjee, thank you all so much for your amazing feedback, critique and contributions. Your support is truly appreciated. Thank you all. You are appreciated.

Annie Chae and Charlotte Christiaanse: thank you for your ground-breaking work on competitor intelligence and battlecards; you are really ahead of your time, I cannot wait to see how the industry embraces battlecards over the next decade. Leila Mortet, thank you for your amazing work on cultural intelligence within Talent Intelligence, you are forging new ground and challenging the status quo, don't ever stop. Marlieke Pols, thank you for all you do in this industry, from standing up entirely new offerings such as Always on Intelligence with Sapna Bhagat and Priyaranjan Dhar, to crafting one of the world's first white papers on Talent Intelligence. You are a powerhouse in this industry and will continue to be in the future. Gerrit Schimmelpenninck and Anastasiia Kolos, thank you for all your work driving and inventing in the M&A Intelligence space; I firmly believe this can be one of the most impactful, and yet currently under-served, areas of Talent Intelligence.

Mike Sandiford and the team at Horsefly Analytics, thank you for all you do with the community. You are always open to help and support and thank you for the insights in this book around the increase in incidence rates of talent intelligence in the job market. I couldn't have done it without you.

To my bosses over the last decade, thank you for trusting me to explore and experiment and bring some of these ideas to life. Cynthia Burkhardt and Alan Agnew: without your vision and empowerment I would never have been able to build what we did at Philips, a period that has influenced many elements written within here and for that I thank you. To my Amazon leaders old and new, Shannon Miller, Greg Arendt, Dan Wilson, Andrew Willingham, Michael Foster, thank you for trusting me to build out and experiment as we are. I am hugely excited about the potential and what this team can build in the future.

To my teams over the last decade, you make all of this possible. To a person you are some of the smartest, bravest and most inspirational people I know! Priyaranjan Dhar looking at Data Science within Talent Intelligence in a novel and newly-created way. Andre Bradshaw with his entirely unique, and extraordinary, approach to data-focused problem solving (in all facets of life). Or the many amazing individuals not already mentioned, without whom none of this building is possible: Kumar Vaibhav, Abhinandan Choudhury, David Papp, Rishav Chaliha, Mario García, Saifali Dalvi, Syed Haaris, Natasha Paul, Gianmaria Foschini, Elisabeth Wiltens, Samuele Mola, Jingxian Liu, Anouk Fülöp, Raul Armendariz, Chris Acton, Daniel Wilson, Daysi Prieto, Elizabeth Winup, James Jones, Shruti Bathia, Agnes Jeong, Grant Ciuba, Vallari Pai… the list is ongoing but know you have all been absolutely instrumental in the teams we have built out together, without which this book would never have happened. A few have moved on into jobs away from Talent Intelligence (I did warn about this in the career pathing chapter after all), but happily many of you remain in the field doing wonderful things.

Dr John Sullivan, for me you are one of the most impactful writers of this era. You are one of the smartest and sharpest commentators on this industry, thank you.

Josh Bersin, for the last 20-plus years you have been raising the bar across the HR industry. Arguably no single person has had such a wide impact. Thank you for all your time and energies, I am excited to see how you wrap your arms around Workforce Intelligence and see how things develop.

Last, but by no means least, Anne-Marie Heeney, my Development Editor. I left you until last as I knew you would be reading this to the end. Thank you for all you have done. This book wouldn't have happened without you and your guidance. You kept me on the straight and narrow and pulled me kicking and screaming over the finishing line. Thank you for all your support.

I know I will have forgotten some people; for this my humble apologies, you may be aware my memory is not what it should be.

Thank you to you all. Without you all this would never have happened.

Introduction

Beware of the moonwalking bear!

In 2008, Transport for London launched a campaign to increase road safety and awareness of cyclists. The short, minute-long video was simply called 'Awareness Test' and was launched in cinemas across the country before moving online; at the point of me writing, this has been seen over 25 million times on YouTube. It begins by asking the viewer to count the number of passes in a short basketball set-up with two teams wearing white and black respectively. Due to the viewer concentration and focus on the ball moving quickly across the field of vision, they completely miss a person dressed in a bear suit who moonwalks across the screen, across the field of vision and right through the middle of the two teams. The viewer is told about the bear and shown the clip again, followed by the road safety message 'Look out for cyclists'. For over a decade, this campaign, and the parallel concept of blind spots within the business world, have been in my mind.

A blind spot is an area in your range of vision that you cannot see properly but which you really should be able to see, and as PwC highlighted: 'Your brain is on autopilot. Experts tell us that our unconscious mind makes a majority of our decisions. It creates blind spots – unconscious biases that can narrow your vision and potentially influence your behaviours.' These two points caused me to question whether we are doing enough for our leaders to highlight these blind spots and to mitigate the risks on the decisions our leaders are making.

How often are we focused too much on the overt activity, on the areas we have been asked to concentrate on, on the loud and obvious? How often are leaders making decisions based on gut feel, with their brain on autopilot? How often are decisions based on 'gut feel' or hearsay all while we are missing the moonwalking bear through our organizations? What are those moonwalking bears, and what are those blind spots, in a business context and how can they be mitigated through effective labour market and talent intelligence?

Through this book we are going to dig into what exactly Talent Intelligence is. What are the various forms of intelligence gathering and the ethics surrounding the data gathering? What is the difference between talent intelligence and HR Analytics (among others)? How do you practically get started in talent intelligence, spot the red flags and build a business case? What are the types of projects we can expect to support? What are the metrics for success and how do we measure and capture these? Where should I site a talent intelligence function within my organization? What does a talent intelligence maturity journey look like? What sort of tools and resources are available within my organization and in the external landscape? What are the various ways I could look to structure my talent intelligence function? What roles would I have in a talent intelligence function and what would career paths look like? What companies are already doing this work and what does 'good' look like? Before looking to the future, and looking into my crystal ball, let us consider: what is the future of the talent intelligence industry and the talent intelligence function?

01

Context

Before we dive into the details of how to build a talent intelligence muscle in your teams or organizations, it is important that we frame what talent intelligence is, why it is needed and how it evolved into the capability that we see today.

What is Talent Intelligence?

Broadly speaking, there are two definitions of Talent Intelligence that have been created by two different camps.

The often-cited definition of Talent Intelligence by talent intelligence practitioners is:

> Talent Intelligence is the application of external data relating to people, skills, jobs, functions, competitors and geographies to drive business decisions.

This is widely accepted by most talent intelligence practitioners as the most appropriate definition. In fact, in a 2021 Talent Intelligence Collective Benchmarking survey[1] over 80 per cent of survey respondents, of which 73 per cent were practitioners and end users, 16 per cent were external research and talent advisory firms and the remaining 11 per cent were vendors and platform, agreed with this definition with no alterations. However, I would argue that this definition is not broad enough and does not encompass the broader vendor ecosystem.

In 'The Rise of Talent Intelligence' by Talent Tech Labs[2] they define it as:

> the term Talent Intelligence broadly describes the tools and technology platforms that apply AI to the vast quantity of data that lives in companies' hiring systems, as well as data that lives on the open web, to provide a holistic view of candidates and help clients make better strategic decisions around talent.

Although broadly I would agree with this definition, I think restricting the definition to tools and technology platforms as well as the use of AI neglects a huge number of talent intelligence practitioners, and facets of talent intelligence, that they can cover.

Other vendors see the definition slightly differently; one example of that is the talent platform Eightfold.

Eightfold describes itself as being a 'deep-learning talent intelligence platform … powered by the largest global talent data set to unleash the full potential of the total workforce – employees, candidates, contractors, and citizens.' Eightfold's technology 'not only delivers a comprehensive understanding of workforce capabilities, but also understands each individual's capabilities, skills adjacencies, and demonstrated learnability to provide a concrete, future orientation to talent strategy.'[3] As Todd Raphael, Eightfold's Head of Content, put it:

> Talent intelligence – it's about using artificial intelligence to make better decisions throughout the whole employee lifecycle. What's changed a lot is a couple of years ago, customers and potential customers were mostly thinking of it in terms of hiring and sourcing. Now they're looking at better intelligence for things like managing contingent workers. Matching employees with new jobs internally so they don't quit for new jobs … talent intelligence is the ability through technology to better understand talent and people's career potential, … talent intelligence is AI-driven insights into the future.

So, within these definitions, I can see some rather stark conflicts with the vendor ecosystem, seeing that talent intelligence is very much focused on the talent lifecycle and the use of technology to transform the usually internal data within this lifecycle, whereas talent intelligence practitioners have a deeper focus on the application of external labour market data and insights to drive business decisions.

Given this conflict of definition, I would argue a more unified, holistic definition is needed and I would propose be the following:

> Talent Intelligence is the augmentation of internal and external people data with the application of technology, science, insights and intelligence relating to people, skills, jobs, functions, competitors and geographies to drive business decisions.

There is also the overarching use of the term 'talent intelligence' to consider. Is it a team, a function or an action? Arguably, it depends on the context. I would suggest that the following is applicable:

Proper noun:

The function, industry, platforms and field we refer to as Talent Intelligence.

- 'The Talent Intelligence function can use data science to produce strategic insights.'
- 'The senior leadership team have invested in a holistic Talent Intelligence platform to have insights across their full HR ecosystem.'

Noun:

The output and deliverable of talent intelligence.

- 'The Talent Acquisition and Workforce Planning teams have created specific talent intelligence reports highlighting critical skills gaps in the future and the gap with the external market.'

Verb:

The action and process of talent intelligence.

- 'By completing targeted talent intelligence, we have been able to unearth our competitor organizational structures and go to market strategies.'

Throughout this book, you will see me use the term 'talent intelligence' as both a verb and a noun as well as 'Talent Intelligence' as a proper noun, as the function or centre of excellence that completes the talent intelligence activities and produces the talent intelligence reports or dashboards. This may seem like semantics but I think it is important to be clear about the phrase and what we mean by it. There is already a lot of confusion in the definition and the use of 'Talent Intelligence' across the industry, so having some clear guidelines is beneficial.

As we will discuss later, the ways in which this data is collected, stored, analysed, augmented, merged and displayed can vary dramatically, as can the use of this data and the customer base. But at its heart, it is using external labour market data to drive the strategy of, assess the feasibility of and de-risk decisions within organizations.

Why is Talent Intelligence needed?

Since the PwC CEO surveys started in 2008, the availability of key skills has been a primary or the primary concern every year and it has been a growing concern year-on-year since 2009.[4] The surveys highlight that this is not the time or place for small incremental change but rather, given the magnitude of the challenges and uncertainty we are facing, a full rethink of our talent strategies is needed. This will only have been magnified due to the effects of the challenging labour market we have seen in the wake of the Covid 19 outbreak. How we work, where we work and in what relationship to the employer we work is all being redefined and effective talent intelligence can play a key part of helping drive this change.

The biggest concern highlighted by this work by PwC though was that only 34 per cent of CEOs felt that HR were well prepared for the challenges ahead. Meanwhile, even before Covid 19, a 2018 KornFerry study predicted that we would see dramatic global labour shortages of over 85 million skilled workers by 2030. This would then result in lost revenue opportunities of $8.452 trillion, which for context is the combined GDP of Germany and Japan.[5] This rapid period of talent redistribution during and post the Covid pandemic has most likely increased the velocity of this labour shortage and talent mismatch.

Talent intelligence is particularly powerful in times of change, during which decisive, data-backed decision-making becomes vital. Certainly, we are in one of those times now as a mix of different trends and forces impact business. An underlying skills gap may make this worse as companies slowly start to resume activity. It may even be exacerbated by the increased rate of digital transformation that the pandemic has enforced.

And there's a lot of digital transformation happening. Jared Spataro, corporate vice president for Company X 365, wrote:

> In April, we saw more than 200 million Company X Teams meeting participants in a single day, generating more than 4.1 billion meeting minutes. Also, Teams now has more than 75 million daily active users … In this era of remote everything, we have seen two years' worth of digital transformation in two months.

All this change and transformation has meant that organizations have had to pivot at a rate never before seen. Consequently, companies are entering new territory as they look for skills that they have not needed historically.

With all this change comes opportunity. Talent leaders have an opportunity to be centre stage and to genuinely influence strategy and business direction like never before. Talent functions can really influence whether their organizations flourish or struggle to survive post-Covid.

With this context of demand and an increase of aggregated external labour market data vendors (to be discussed later), we have seen a rapid increase in the number of specialist talent intelligence functions being formed within organizations.

A brief history of Talent Intelligence

So now that we have a handle on what we mean by Talent Intelligence and have some guardrails around the definition we are using to frame the conversation, it is now important to understand how we have found ourselves in the current state. Why hasn't Talent Intelligence been around longer? Why is it appearing so much now? Is this really something new or just a rebranding of existing capabilities?

In researching this book I've seen that Talent Intelligence as a term has been used sporadically since the mid-1990s. In the early years it was largely referring to analytics and intelligence on your own internal 'talent'. Your workforce. At the time, this was largely done by HR analytics professionals with a view to improving talent management. This itself was a new function at the time with McKinsey driving home the concept in their 1997 paper and the 2001 book on *The War for Talent*. The phrase never really took off though and it wasn't really for another 10 years that Talent Intelligence really started to make a comeback as a term and often with newly-changed focus and direction. The reason for this could be debated but, in my mind, the clearest trigger was the emergence of the macro aggregating labour market vendors, spearheaded by the likes of:

- BurningGlass (founded in 1999)
- Wanted Analytics (founded in 1999)
- EMSI (founded in 2000)

Then with a second wave with:

- JobstheWord/Horsefly Analytics (founded in 2011)
- Talent Neuron (founded in 2012)
- Humantelligence (founded in 2013)
- Claro Analytics (formed in 2014)

- Restless Bandit (formed in 2014)
- Draup (founded in 2017)
- Stratigens (founded in 2018)
- LinkedIn Talent Insights (launched in 2018)
- TalentUp.io (founded in 2018)

This list is not exhaustive and does not includ some of the intelligent sourcing or talent management platforms such as hireEZ, SeekOut, Eightfold AI, Entelo, HiringSolved or Fetcher.

With the broader global talent management software market size of US $6.45 billion in 2020[6], projected to grow from $7.02 billion in 2021 to $13.21 billion in 2028 at a compound annual growth rate (CAGR) of 9.4 per cent in the forecast period,[7] it is no surprise that in parallel to this we have seen the emergence of Talent Intelligence platforms looking to bridge HR/People Analytics and Talent Management.

This boom has given talent intelligence practitioners, HR, recruiters, vendors, intelligence functions and research and consulting firms access to aggregated and often pre-analysed data in a way that we simply have never seen before. This has drastically reduced the technical barrier to entry versus having raw data sets from the various macro data bodies, such as the US Bureau of Labor Statistics and International Labour Organization, and enabled, and continues to enable, far wider and deeper adoption.

Horsefly Analytics highlighted this growth in the appearance of Talent Intelligence within CVs over this period of rapid technological and platform growth.[8] In Figure 1.1 we can see a clear uptick in the frequency of the term as more platforms were built. Now, whether this is being used as a noun or a verb or whether this is simply a trend and a rebranding of other more traditional recruitment or sourcing is up for debate, and we will discuss this later in Chapter 11. This uptick is especially marked and noticeable in the jump from 2017 to 2019 in correlation with the second wave of talent and labour market intelligence products entering the market.

But then something unplanned happened. Covid 19 rocked the world. The world faced a flattening of the labour market in 2020 with mass furloughs and redundancies, with only a few organizations in growth mode. This meant that the growth rate for talent intelligence as a new role type, or even a need within roles, began to plateau. Then in 2021 we saw unprecedented growth in the labour market. Companies bounced back more aggressively than anyone could have predicted. As we can see in Figure 1.2,

FIGURE 1.1   Trend analysis of Talent Intelligence within the marketplace

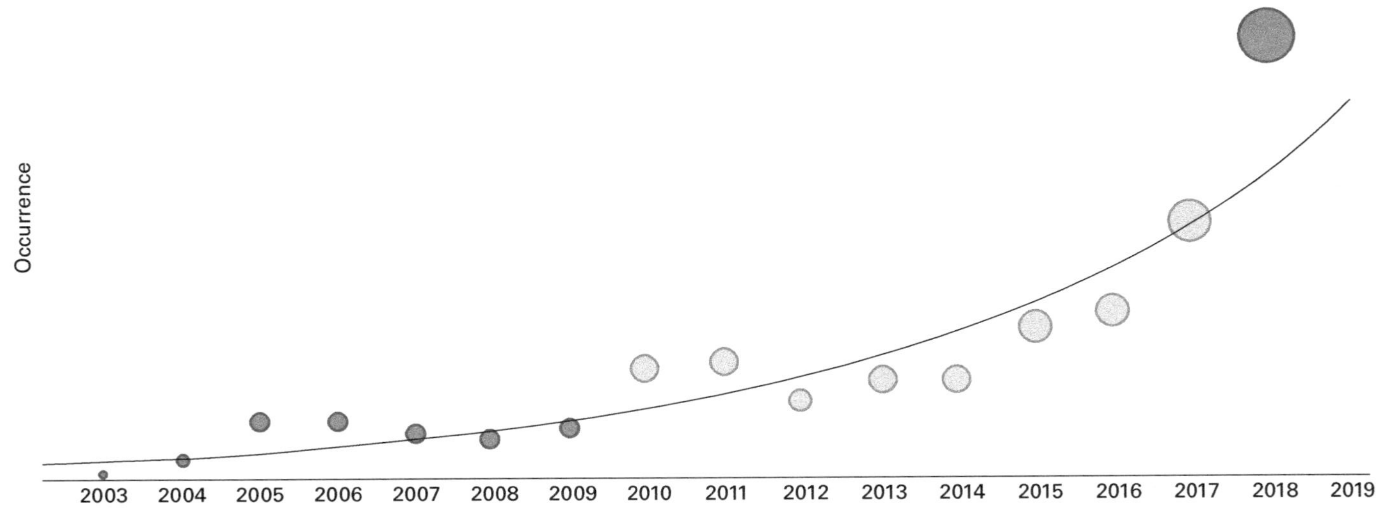

Occurrence

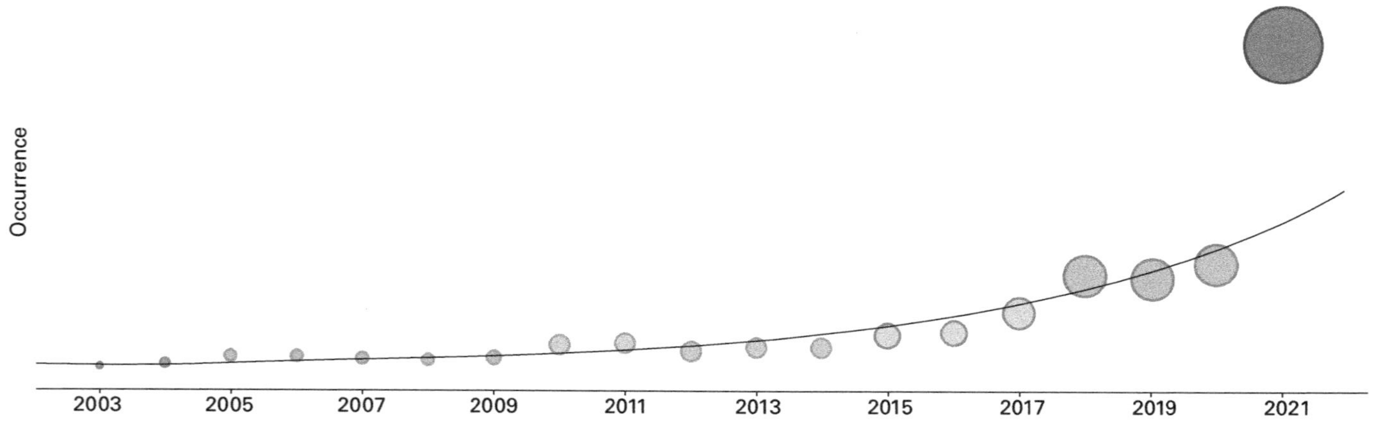

FIGURE 1.2 Trend analysis of Talent Intelligence within the marketplace, updated for 2021

this was mirrored in the explosive increase in the frequency of talent intelligence appearing in job adverts. Suddenly the world was struggling to find the talent they needed and were looking for labour market expertise to help guide them through this period.

Through this we have seen two major trends: the first a drastic uptick in the number of more traditional sourcing and recruiting roles with an element of intelligence incorporated into the responsibilities; and the second in the formation of whole new talent intelligence specific roles and functions. In fact, in the 2021 Talent Intelligence Collective Benchmarking study of 51 organizations, over 50 per cent of all respondents said their teams had been created in the last 2 years, with a further 8 per cent saying they were in the process of carving out a new function/team for Talent Intelligence.[9]

Summary

Talent intelligence is the augmentation of internal and external people data with the application of technology, science, insights and intelligence relating to people, skills, jobs, functions, competitors and geographies to drive business decisions. This capability has been enabled by an increase in labour market data visibility, quality and aggregation that enabled a vendor technology landscape to flourish. This technology, coupled with an increased labour market competition and volatility, has triggered a sharp increase in the need for labour market intelligence as never before. This is still early days for talent intelligence and this capability and function will continue to grow and develop, as we will discuss later in this book.

TOBY'S TAKEAWAYS

- Talent intelligence is a new and as yet undefined field that we have the power to shape and mould.
- There has never been a more relevant time in the workforce to launch a talent intelligence capability.
- Demand is heavily growing for talent intelligence individuals. As we will discuss in Chapter 17, creating future talent intelligence capabilities and pipelines of talent will be key for growth.

Endnotes

1 The Talent Intelligence Collective 2021 Benchmarking Survey. See resources from the Talent Intelligence Collective at: www.koganpage.com/talent-intelligence (archived at https://perma.cc/XFZ7-3AAC).

2 TTL (2021) 'The Rise of Talent Intelligence: TTL's trend report', talenttechlabs.com/blog/the-rise-of-talent-intelligence-trend-report/ (archived at https://perma.cc/AT3C-FVC3)

3 Eightfold (no date), eightfold.ai/why-eightfold/talent-intelligence-platform/ (archived at https://perma.cc/AT3C-FVC3)

4 PwC (2014) 'The Talent Challenge: Adapting to growth', www.pwc.com/gx/en/services/people-organisation/publications/ceosurvey-talent-challenge.html (archived at https://perma.cc/JL3H-9GT4)

5 KornFerry (2018) 'Future of Work: The Global Talent Crunch', www.kornferry.com/content/dam/kornferry/docs/pdfs/KF-Future-of-Work-Talent-Crunch-Report.pdf (archived at https://perma.cc/T9GW-B7H8)

6 Fortune Business Insights (2021) 'Fortune Business Insights Report: Talent management software market size, share & Covid 19 impact analysis', May, www.fortunebusinessinsights.com/ (archived at https://perma.cc/YE2D-827L)

7 Ibid.

8 M Pols (2019) 'Talent Intelligence Why, what and how: A guide to commercially successful Talent Intelligence in a digital era', www.armstrongcraven.com/uploads/talent_intelligence_why_what_and_how_a_guide_to_commercially_successful_talent_inte2.pdf (archived at https://perma.cc/42Y5-E26H)

9 The Talent Intelligence Collective 2021 Benchmarking Survey. See resources from the Talent Intelligence Collective at: www.koganpage.com/talent-intelligence (archived at https://perma.cc/XFZ7-3AAC).

02

Types of intelligence

So now that we know what we mean by talent intelligence, and also know how we have arrived at the current state from a vendor and landscape evolution, let us dive into the wonderful world of intelligence. First, let us be very clear – there will be far more data available to you than you will be able to handle, so be selective. Estimates suggest that at least 2.5 quintillion bytes of data is produced every day. That is 2,500,000,000,000,000,000 bytes and, according to projections from Statista, 74 zettabytes of data were created in 2021 – 74,000,000,000,000,000,000,000 bytes. For context, in 2018, the total amount of data created, captured, copied and consumed in the world was 33 zettabytes. So in a three-year window, data production has more than doubled.

As Melvin Vopson said: 'To help visualise these numbers, let's imagine that each bit is a £1 coin, which is around 3 mm (0.1 inches) thick. One ZB made up of a stack of coins would be 2,550 light years. This can get you to the nearest star system, Alpha Centauri, 600 times.' [1]

The 74 ZB that we produce will take our stack of £1 coins to 188,700 light years, which is nearly double the diameter of the Milky Way galaxy (105,700 light years) or we could take 7.5 trips to Hercules Globular (M 13), which is a mere 25,000 light years.

The reason I highlight this is because accessing data has never been easier. As we will discuss in more detail in Chapter 9, you will have or will be able to generate more data on the labour market, specific talent within it or your internal population than you will ever need. Keep mindful of what is needed, what is appropriate and how this data is processed, stored and used.

To truly understand how to capture this data for talent intelligence it is important to understand the larger context of the intelligence landscape and that is what we are going to explore in this chapter.

What are the types of intelligence?

At a macro level, there is a broad range of intelligence-gathering disciplines. Many of these are used in the military, police services, security services, threat intelligence and so on, but some are also very relevant to the work that we are doing within Talent Intelligence. In this section we will look at all the core intelligence disciplines but be conscious that not all will immediately translate into the world of talent intelligence.

SIGINT

Signals Intelligence (SIGINT) is 'intelligence derived from electronic signals and systems used by foreign targets, such as communications systems, radars, and weapons systems. SIGINT provides a vital window... into foreign adversaries' capabilities, actions, and intentions'.[2] Of all the intelligence disciplines, SIGINT is the least likely to be directly relevant to your talent intelligence offerings – given the nature of the data-gathering techniques and the data output. Having said this, the principle of long-range threat detection does have an interesting overlay into the world of talent intelligence as we will discuss in Chapter 5.

IMINT

Imagery Intelligence (IMINT) 'includes representations of objects reproduced electronically or by optical means on film, electronic display devices, or other media. Imagery can be derived from visual photography, radar sensors, infrared sensors, lasers, and electro-optics'. [3]

GEOINT

Geospatial Intelligence (GEOINT) is intelligence about the human activity on earth derived from the exploitation and analysis of imagery and geospatial information that describes, assesses and visually depicts physical features and geographically referenced activities on the Earth.[4] Within GEOINT you also find MASINT, which is Measurement and Signature Intelligence, and Geospatial Information and Services (GIS).

Although GEOINT and IMINT do not directly translate into the world of talent intelligence, there could certainly be some interesting parallels. For example, if you look into targeted location intelligence or sourcing activities, competitor site expansion, competitor facilities and soft office benefits from images online.

CYBINT/DNINT

Cyber or Digital Network Intelligence (CYBINT or DNINT) is the process of explicitly gaining intelligence from available resources on the internet. CYBINT can often be considered as a subset of OSINT.[5]

HUMINT

Human Intelligence (HUMINT) is intelligence gathered by means of personal contact. Essentially, it is a category of intelligence derived from information collected and provided by human sources. This separates it from the other forms of intelligence that are more technical intelligence gathering disciplines.

The Intelligence Officers who conduct HUMINT activities are best known for their role in recruiting Covert Human Intelligence Sources (CHIS) – or, as they are more commonly known to the public, criminal informers[6] recruiting spies and foreign informants – they also routinely collect and report information from friendly forces, civilians, refugees and local inhabitants.

In a study of HUMINT within the police force, 24 police handlers were interviewed. They largely agreed that the ability to build rapport and relationships could be trained to some degree and that rapport was not viewed exclusively as a natural skill. It was noted, however, that participants commonly perceived some natural attributes were required to build rapport that could be refined and developed through training and experience.[7]

These elements can be very relevant for Talent Intelligence and have direct parallels to the work we do. Let's dig into these in a little more detail.

HOW HUMINT IS RELEVANT FOR TALENT INTELLIGENCE

Some of the core skills needed for effective rapport building are: finding common ground, creating shared experiences, keeping the focus on the target/candidate by asking relevant questions and listening to their response, being empathic, mirroring and matching mannerisms and speech appropriately. This is the cornerstone of effective talent acquisition interviewing and this can be leveraged within our Talent Intelligence world.

Through every interview and candidate interaction, we have the opportunity to acquire data in a manner and scale that is unique within our organizations. No other function will talk to as many individuals from competitor companies. No other function has the access and ability to ask probing and challenging questions about the work the competitor does, their structure, their design, their impact. As Dr John Sullivan put it in his excellent 2019 article 'Recruiting's Missed Strategic Opportunity – Competitive Intelligence Gathering':

> During a job interview with a competitor's employee, they mention working on a brand-new product. Would this fact be reported to your product managers? Unfortunately, probably not. Despite the fact that during normal activities, recruiters routinely discover valuable business information about their firm's competitors, few TA functions have a formal process for gathering or reporting this information to their own managers that could put this information to immediate use. Not having a competitive intelligence (aka CI) gathering process is a missed opportunity for recruiting to increase its strategic contribution and its direct business impacts.[8]

There are two main routes to look into building this competitive intelligence muscle within TA/Executive Recruitment: the first is a surgical approach, the second a macro-scaled approach. Building out a systematic, scaled competitor intelligence approach to encompass all of Talent Acquisition is difficult. Ensuring the data capture – whether this is from an interview process or through a CV review – is accurate and validated, legal and compliant, stored in a secure environment, surfaced, processed and analysed effectively and so on, is a huge challenge. With that in mind, many can look to a more targeted and surgical approach by focusing on specific individuals in an interview process from specific competitors and injecting pre-prepared intelligence questions into the interview process. This is powerful in a number of functions that you will interview for across the organization, including:

- in technical fields to understand competitor R&D
- in sales or marketing to better understand go to market strategies or launch planning
- in IT to understand the underlying infrastructure and possible future organizational pivots

- even into Talent Acquisition to see early predictors of future growth or restructuring, but this can be especially impactful when tied in to Executive Recruitment. Having the ability to tie strategic intelligence needs gathering into existing or forecast executive talent scouting and talent pipelining is potentially a huge strategic competitive advantage to an organization

Using these moments of leadership transparency can help gain insight into:

- the leadership style of a competitor
- a competitor's future strategy
- competitor attrition or talent challenges they are facing
- investment or growth plans of a competitor
- a competitor's remuneration strategy or their sales compensation schemes and effectiveness
- what technologies a competitor is investing into
- how a competitor is pivoting or transforming as an organization, etc.

These are all elements that are routinely discussed and probed via an executive search process, but rarely are these competitor insights surfaced through the organization to the relevant decision makers from a strategic perspective. It is important throughout this to really think about the ethics of your activity.

OSINT

Open Source Intelligence (OSINT) is defined by both the US Director of National Intelligence and the US Department of Defense (DoD) as intelligence 'produced from publicly available information that is collected, exploited, and disseminated in a timely manner to an appropriate audience for the purpose of addressing a specific intelligence'.[9] OSINT is an area that has a natural home within the talent acquisition and, more specifically, the sourcing, research and talent intelligence worlds. At its heart it is about finding information from online sources and distilling that down to give clear data points. That could be online personal contact information; it could be a blog, a CV, a social profile; it could be a job description, a company report or a company's board of director's page. The potential sources are limitless and how they can be used within Talent Intelligence is only limited by your imagination.

OSINT WORKED EXAMPLE

For example, you have been asked to dig into a competitor company as a potential target for acquisition or for benchmarking purposes. The brief is broad: you are looking to understand their workforce, their leadership team, their hiring practices, where they are investing, what their organizational functional design is and their diversity performance. At first this feels overwhelming. Where do you even start? The good news is there are lots of sources out there that can give you areas to dive into; for example, you may find some of the following:

- From their company website:
  o executive committee/board leadership
  o management teams
  o organization structures
  o new product launches
- News:
  o product launches, downsizing
  o investment
  o executive movement announcements
- Job adverts/job descriptions:
  o hiring changes
  o company pivots
  o new market entry
  o roles and remits
- LinkedIn:
  o organization structures
  o roles and remits
  o size and scale levelling

In Chapter 5 we will look at this through a worked example, in order to dig into this a little more and put some meat on these bones.

Data policies/GDPR

By its very nature, often when looking at OSINT you will have a large amount of personally identifiable information that is unearthed. If you are going to store and process this information, and if it is likely that you as the researcher or the target you are researching is within the EU, you will need to be mindful of GDPR compliance.

The key GDPR aspects for OSINT researchers to consider are that you must:

- be accountable
- make sure you have a legal basis for processing personal data
- apply the key principles in the processing of personal data
- understand, anticipate and honour the rights of the data subject
- understand if you are the data controller or the data processor

Data ethics

Data ethics refers to moral obligation and the associated systemizing, defending and recommending concepts of right and wrong conduct in relation to data, in particular personal data.[10] As Harvard professor Dustin Tingley puts it, 'data ethics asks, "Is this the right thing to do?" and "Can we do better?"'[11]

Gartner have suggested a further '7 Guiding Principles for Data Ethics in HR' and the following principles to 'take the lead on data ethics and establish employee trust in the company's ethical use of their data'.[12] We can equally use these principles as a starting point to mirror across to broader external labour market data as well as the internal population. Let's dive into these '7 Guiding Principles for Data Ethics in HR' from a talent intelligence lens:

1 Understand your company's data ethics comfort zone. Through their Global Labour Market Survey (1Q19), Gartner saw that only 4 per cent of employees were unwilling to share any category of data, whereas each category had a very different willingness to share, especially if employees understood the benefits in doing so. This is also worth thinking about with reference to external labour market data. What is your targeted labour market willing to share? What would they feel is appropriate? Do they understand the benefits in sharing this data?

2   Articulate a data ethics code that is grounded in your organizational culture. Be clear and transparent about your ethics code and how it aligns with your organizational culture, values and tenets. This will enable you to set clear boundaries as to how you capture, process or use data while ensuring you are not restricting but rather enabling the organization to flourish.

3   Identify and learn from key partners. This is vital to remember. Talent analytics/intelligence leaders **do not** need to be subject matter experts in all areas. Partner with others in the organization, whether this is legal, data privacy, IT, competitive intelligence, marketing intelligence, compliance, etc., to share lessons and best practices, risk mitigation and data ethics alignment across your organization.

4   Mandate clarity of purpose and intent for any project that uses employee data. As with all data use, be clear about what you are collecting and limiting your data collecting to the bare minimum needed for the desired outcome.

5   Communicate the 'what' and 'why' to employees. Transparency is key whenever you are processing data. Build this transparency into any working model as early as possible to help build trust with your stakeholders.

6   Give employees more control over their data. For internal employees, it is key to allow them access and control of their data – allow them to opt in or out of data collection initiatives as desired. This shared ownership and shared control will also increase the quality of the data within the HR systems as employees feel empowered to own their data. This does, however, pose more challenges with external data, especially with the lens of GDPR and legitimate interest.

7   Solicit employee feedback and continually audit your data policies. Creating a safe mechanism and feedback loop is key to building trust, transparency and a shared ownership across the organization. This mechanism is key to continually improve the quality, accuracy and robustness of the data sets you are looking to build.

Core principles

Although in the above we can look at elements of this HR data ethics framework with respect to talent intelligence, I would argue that due to the nature of the data gathered in broader talent and labour market intelligence, it is also necessary to look at a broader contextual framework. Harvard have suggested five broader data ethics core principles.[13] These are:

1 Ownership/consent

2 Transparency

3 Privacy

4 Intention

5 Outcomes

Let us look at these in order.

1 OWNERSHIP

Ownership and consent are widely considered the first principle of data ethics in that an individual should have full ownership over their personal information and give consent as to how the information is gathered, stored and processed. It is unlawful and unethical to collect someone's personal data without their consent. More specifically, within the GDPR framework, processing personal data is generally prohibited, unless it is expressly allowed by law, or the data subject has consented to the processing. Consent must be freely given, specific, informed and unambiguous. In order to obtain freely given consent, it must be given on a voluntary basis.[14]

The general consensus is to never assume an individual is comfortable with you collecting their data; always ask for permission to avoid ethical and legal dilemmas. This can lead to some difficult situations, however, when dealing with data relating to talent mapping in situations such as executive research. Even with publicly available data, whether on social platforms such as LinkedIn, where data is published under a user agreement and privacy policy between the user and social network, or more broadly with OSINT data, it is important to remember that anyone looking to store and process that data would still need to demonstrate a lawful basis for processing and obtain consent from the individuals in question.

2 TRANSPARENCY

For consent to be informed and specific, the data subject must at least be notified about the controller's identity, what kind of data will be processed, how it will be used and the purpose of the processing operations as a safeguard against 'function creep'.[15] It is a user's right to have access to this information so they can decide to accept your needs and grant consent or not. The importance of transparency cannot be underestimated – lying about your methods or intentions is deception and both unlawful and unfair to your data subjects.

3 PRIVACY

Even if you are given consent by a customer to collect, store and analyse their personally identifiable information (PII), that does not mean they want it publicly available. This means you have an ethical responsibility that comes with handling data in ensuring data subjects' privacy.

No matter what your security precautions, mistakes can still be made by professionals who regularly handle and analyse sensitive data. For the use within talent intelligence, one way to mitigate this risk is de-identifying a dataset. A dataset is de-identified when all pieces of PII are removed, leaving only anonymous data. This enables analysts to find relationships between variables of interest without attaching specific data points to individual identities.

4 INTENTION

Let's be very clear, intentions matter. Before collecting data, ask yourself why you need it, what you will gain from it and what changes you will be able to make after analysis. If you are not comfortable with the answers, then you really need to question whether it is needed or ethical. If your intention is to hurt others, profit from your subjects' weaknesses or any other malicious goal, it is not ethical to collect their data.

Even when your intentions are good – for instance, collecting data to reduce age discrimination/improving diversity across your organization by creating an aggregated tool – you should still assess your intention behind the collection of each piece of data and how things could go wrong.

Do you really need all the data points you are asking for? Strive to collect the minimum viable amount of data, so that you are taking as little as possible from your subjects while making a difference.

5 OUTCOMES

Even when intentions are good, we need to be very conscious of potential disparate impact. Disparate impact is often referred to as 'unintentional discrimination', whereas disparate treatment is intentional. The outcome of data analysis can cause inadvertent harm to individuals or groups of people. Sadly, it can be very hard to know the potential disparate impact until the analysis is done and the outcomes are presented, but it is important to consider this as much as possible beforehand. Do not only consider the best-case scenario; think about what would happen if this tool or analysis was used inappropriately and look for ways to mitigate that risk.

Summary

The concepts of intelligence are new to this area. Be open-minded and look at opportunities for data gathering across your workflow and landscape, but do so in a deliberate and ethical manner. You will have access to more data than you will imagine and more than you will need; resist the temptation to simply capture all. Look at alternative fields of study with more mature intelligence offerings and see where parallels can be drawn, even if non-direct. Ensure you are strong and processing all data in an ethical and legal manner. I would highly recommend engaging with your internal legal teams early in any data-gathering process to ensure that you are remaining compliant.

TOBY'S TAKEAWAYS

- There is more data available on the labour market than ever before, but it is largely still highly unstructured and messy.
- There is a broad range of both primary and secondary intelligence-gathering disciplines used to gather this data.
- Just because you can, it doesn't mean you should. Be very clear about the ethical standards you expect from your talent intelligence offering.

Endnotes

1 M M Vopson (2021) 'The World's Data Explained: How much we're producing and where it's all stored', *The Conversation*, 4 May, theconversation.com/the-worlds-data-explained-how-much-were-producing-and-where-its-all-stored-159964 (archived at https://perma.cc/HL4M-WHN8)

2 NSA/CSS (no date) 'Collecting & Analyzing Our Adversaries' Moves', www.nsa.gov/Signals-Intelligence/ (archived at https://perma.cc/EJK4-83M5)

3 INTEL (no date) www.intelligence.gov/ (archived at https://perma.cc/DR88-ARPK)

4 (no date) GEOINT – Geospatial Intelligence, www.heavy.ai/technical-glossary/ geoint (archived at https://perma.cc/P87J-788M)

5 K Rein (2013) 'Re-thinking Standardization for Interagency Information Sharing', in B. Akhgar and S. Yates (eds) *Strategic Intelligence Management*, Butterworth-Heinemann, pp. 199–211.

6 C Crous (2009) 'Human Intelligence Sources: Challenges in Policy Development', *Security Challenges* Vol. 5, No. 3 (Spring), pp. 117–127, DOI: 10.1016/B978-0-12-407191-9.00016-8.

7 J Nunan, I Stanier, R Milne, A Shawyer, D Walsh (2020) 'Eliciting human intelligence: police source handlers' perceptions and experiences of rapport during covert human intelligence sources (CHIS) interactions', *Psychiatry, Psychology and Law*, DOI: 10.1080/13218719.2020.1734978

8 J Sullivan (2019) 'Recruiting's Missed Strategic Opportunity — Competitive Intelligence Gathering', 17 June, drjohnsullivan.com/articles/recruiting-strategy/recruitings-missed-strategic-opportunity-competitive-intelligence-gathering/ (archived at https://perma.cc/2M6J-43XZ)

9 As defined in Sec. 931 of Public Law 109-163, entitled 'National Defense Authorization Act for Fiscal Year 2006'. Archived from the original on 11 December 2008. Retrieved 12 August 2006.

10 R Kitchin (2014) 'The Data Revolution: Big Data, Open Data, Data Infrastructures and Their Consequences', SAGE, 18 August, p. 27.

11 R Kitchin (2021) '5 Principles of Data Ethics for Business', Harvard Business School Online, 16 March, online.hbs.edu/blog/post/data-ethics (archived at https://perma.cc/NTK4-MGU6)

12 Gartner (no date) '7 Guiding Principles for Data Ethics in HR', www.gartner.com/en/human-resources/trends/principles-for-hr-data-ethics (archived at https://perma.cc/8FFQ-385L)

13 C Cote (2021) '5 Principles of Data Ethics for Business', Harvard Business School Online, 16 March, online.hbs.edu/blog/post/data-ethics (archived at https://perma.cc/NTK4-MGU6)

14 GDPR, Article 7 and recital 32, gdpr-info.eu/recitals/no-32/ (archived at https://perma.cc/65S3-RZQC)

15 Intersoft Consulting (no date) 'Consent', gdpr-info.eu/issues/consent/ (archived at https://perma.cc/5NZL-SWG3)

03

The great debate

One of the questions I am most commonly asked is, 'What is the difference between Talent Intelligence and HR analytics?' Closely followed by, 'What is the difference between Talent Intelligence and sourcing intelligence or executive research?' The short answer is that, in my opinion, this is not a clear-cut world. Where they exist in organizations, all these areas and capabilities interact and overlap; it is better to think of what elements you are dialling up or down in a function.

In this chapter, we will look at the various roles and remits of HR analytics, talent acquisition analytics, workforce analytics, talent intelligence, sourcing intelligence and executive recruitment research and see their similarities, crossovers and room for mutual engagement.

But first, let us get some foundations in place for what we are talking about.

HR analytics (HRA)

HR analytics, often also referred to as 'people analytics', is broadly accepted to be the collation, analysis and application of HR- and talent-related data to look to measure, improve and forecast vital talent-related organizational outcomes. HR analytics leaders look to push forward a data-driven HR culture across the function, but especially throughout the HR leadership. The aim is to use data to inform talent decisions, improve workforce planning, talent management and strategic workforce planning processes and promote positive employee experience. It is worth noting here that there is not clarification around whether this talent data is internal or external, only that said data is used to improve critical talent and business outcomes.

HR analytics often captures and measures the functioning of the HR team itself. It is an internally-focused health mechanism analysing key performance indicators (KPIs) such as employee attrition – both voluntary and involuntary, retention rate, employee satisfaction, diversity rates, etc.

People analytics as a term is often used interchangeably with HR analytics. There is still some debate and at times people analytics is used to encompass HR, the entire workforce data and customer insights in a much broader contextual view, to see both the holistic talent and people-related data, but also tying this to core customer data (especially in a B2C environment). This can absolutely look to cross over into the world of both talent intelligence and talent acquisition analytics.

Talent acquisition analytics (TAA)

One element that is often lost in the broader HRA landscape is that of talent acquisition analytics (TAA). TA analytics is the systematic capture, reporting, analysis and discovery of insights in support of decision-making related to recruitment and onboarding processes, activities and outcomes. The three primary categories of measurement (efficiency, effectiveness, impact) are generally leveraged across four types of analysis (descriptive, relative, analytic and predictive) to varying degrees of success and maturity across the market. Within this there are a number of potential subsets whether that is looking at:

- the overall TA organization and capacity planning
- recruitment efficiency (time to hire, cost per hire, etc.)
- recruitment marketing and campaign analytics
- sourcing funnel and channel effectiveness analytics
- candidate experience intelligence, etc.

Workforce analytics (WA)

Workforce analytics is a relatively new term and is usually used to reflect measuring a workforce's productivity, engagement and collaboration. Notably, it encompasses the entire group of workers (not just full-time employees) and allows for the future inclusion of AI and robots that will potentially replace current jobs within an organization. Workforce analytics, therefore, is more descriptive when it comes to making a holistic workforce strategy. WA is traditionally far more business focused than HRA, whether this is directly with the line leadership or through talent management teams. As mentioned, WA is focused on a workforce's productivity, engagement and collaboration, and looking to drive the greatest return on investment on this. This leads to grey areas, as often WA will investigate employee health metrics that directly align with HR Analytics workflows such as:

- retention rates
- employee flight risk
- performance management metrics
- identification of training/skills gaps
- improved demand planning for recruitment efficiency
- reducing bias through the recruitment funnel/promotion process, etc.

Talent Intelligence (TI)

The purpose of this capability is to partner with their customer, whether this is internally or from an external vendor into a client, to allow the organization to scale and respond in an agile manner while mitigating risk and assessing feasibility from a labour market perspective. The definition of 'customer' is broad and open to growth (as we will discuss in Chapter 5), but generally within internal talent intelligence teams, they will initially see talent acquisition, executive recruitment or talent management teams as their customer base and route to market. Within a vendor environment, the customer definition will usually be simply a decision-making authority within a target customer organization. This is usually more aligned to the function they were formed within than the actual defined customer base. Talent intelligence helps their businesses with making smart talent decisions, forward-thinking, evaluating best practices, interpreting labour market data and solidifying and clarifying talent strategies. At its core, it is about using labour market data to de-risk decision-making and strategy processes. Typical talent intelligence questions could be: 'What location could we set up our new development centre in?'; 'We want to merge with this target company, is it feasible to expand their operations in this location by XX per cent?'; 'What is our talent attractiveness in this location?'; 'What are competitors' Employee Value Propositions and how do we compare and compete against these?'

Sourcing intelligence (SI)

Sourcing intelligence enables the application of talent intelligence for sourcing and recruitment teams and programmes, and delivers insights for sourcing and recruitment leaders. Through the use of both internal and external candidate, employer and industry-level data, customers receive both tactical and strategic talent solutions. Questions that can often be addressed by SI are issues such as: 'What talent is in the area and what strategies will mitigate risk?'; 'How can we increase diversity in our talent pipelines?'; 'How can we inform our strategies with historical candidate data?'; 'How are companies hiring and how could it impact our strategies?'

Executive recruitment research (ERR)

Executive recruitment research is the bedrock of any executive recruitment search. This process is about using prior knowledge of the client, the role type, the market and the industry to craft an effective executive recruitment strategy. Depending upon the set-up and organization, some research functions will be strictly in the background. They will be the engine room with recruiters facing off to both candidates and to clients and stakeholders. In other organizations, they will be much more visible – both crafting and leading the search strategy, engaging with prospects and presenting shortlists to the client along with the search partner. SI and ERR often use similar skills and data sets but usually SI is also considering longer term pipeline feasibility of a role, whereas ERR is looking for the niche hire and specific skill and context. Through the process of running such searches, it is vital for the researchers to truly understand the competitor, market, industry and business landscape. Due to this, you will often see teams recycling this research and knowledge into business communications or knowledge hubs to share their broader knowledge of executive talent and competitor trends. This can often be the organization's initial steps into the world of talent intelligence.

Summary of functions and capabilities

In the current state, we see a number of specializations within the entire workforce intelligence arena with a large amount of crossover and confusion between functions, however more commonly it is likely that you will see the following:

- HR analytics looking at HR health and KPIs and metrics supporting that health

- People analytics coming in more broadly, looking at all 'people', so by its nature also potentially looking into customer bases, although the majority of PA functions are primarily at this stage looking internally into their organizations to understand their employee health and organizational health

- Workforce analytics being a more encompassing term for the workforce as a whole, looking at employees, gig workers, freelancers, consultants, etc. But also importantly looking to the future and what the future of the workforce and labour market might look like

- Talent intelligence being primarily being the macro external talent and labour market lens. The augmentation of that external people data and the internal data with the application of technology, science, insights and intelligence relating to people, skills, jobs, functions, competitors and geographies to drive business decisions

- Sourcing intelligence being the micro external talent and labour market lens. This is the drill-through from the helicopter view of talent intelligence to something more actionable on the ground and in real time

- Executive recruitment research being used to improve the efficiency and effectiveness of specific, niche executive search requirements, as well as broader knowledge management and communication for executive talent and competitor trends

Traditionally, drawing a line between HR/people and analytics/workforce analytics versus sourcing/talent and intelligence/executive research shows that the core key difference is between the usage of external and internal data. The former focus on current employees in an organization. They tend to be inward-looking, using internal tools and systems. The latter, on the other hand, focus more on the external market using external data, tools and sources with the clearest bridge being talent acquisition analytics that can span both the internal and external world very comfortably. Although all functions use different approaches, they need to partner together to understand the bigger holistic picture.

How this looks in organizations

Due to the blurry lines between these various groups, they may often integrate, as the required skill sets and target data sets tend to be similar in nature. Many organizations won't have one or many of the above functions. They may have these activities being covered within other groups. They may have many of the above merged into single functions. There is no correct or wrong answer. This is a transformative period for all fields of analytics and intelligence and workforce, labour, HR or talent fields are transforming at an alarming rate. Internally-focused teams are needing to see externally for context of the competitor landscape or labour market. Externally-focused teams are needing to look internally to understand why the organization has the pain points it does, where the bottlenecks are, what the problems are that we are trying to solve, etc.

Summary

So, as we can see, there is a lot of development and growth within the whole human capital analytics and intelligence lifecycle, whether in traditionally externally-focused efforts in talent intelligence, sourcing intelligence or executive recruitment research, or traditionally internally-focused HR analytics, workforce analytics or the merging of those worlds in talent acquisition analytics. All these elements are broadening their scopes and remits and it is very likely we will see continual growth and evolution before we see these functions combining into a more structured HR Science-type function. But, before we jump to the future, let's dig a little more into how it is you can build the business case for talent intelligence capacity or a talent intelligence function.

TOBY'S TAKEAWAYS

- There are many functions and teams looking at human capital intelligence from a number of angles.

- There is a huge amount of overlap between the remits of different teams.

- Often, teams focused on internal data have stronger skills around data analytics and a strong self-service culture while developing consulting skills, whereas teams focused on external data often have the opposite situation, being stronger on consulting and business partnering and are developing their data analytics capabilities. This will be explored more in Chapter 11.

- There is a large opportunity to align, but be mindful of the differences between teams and functions.

04

Building the case for talent intelligence

This chapter is a crowdsourced/crowd-written chapter by the awesome individuals within the Talent Intelligence Collective. A huge thank you to those authors involved in this chapter, especially Jacob Madsen, Lyndon Llanes and James Brown. Thank you all. For the ease of reading and to maintain the narrative, I will use 'I' through this chapter, but the shared voices, experiences and inputs are greatly appreciated.

This chapter will explore what initial warning signs you can see in your organization as triggers to needing talent intelligence support, as well as looking into defining your customer base, looking at your vision, mission and principles, before building out your use cases and looking at how you will build trust across your organization for your Talent Intelligence function.

Talent Intelligence or talent intelligence?

A point to note at this juncture is to be clear about what you are trying to achieve. Is it talent intelligence as a capability within a pre-existing team, as an aside to a multi-threaded team, i.e. talent intelligence as an activity, or are you looking to build out a stand-alone Talent Intelligence function? Both absolutely have their place. Creating a culture of intelligence across a multi-threaded team that will naturally see problems in a more holistic manner is very positive; equally, having a fully dedicated Talent Intelligence function will allow for growth and specialization within the competence.

These are not mutually exclusive events. Many will start with talent intelligence, often projects being run from recruitment marketing, sourcing or recruitment, but also it could be at times from HR analytics, business analytics, marketing intelligence or strategic workforce planning – any function that is aware that the human element is their biggest asset and barrier to success if not accounted for. This initial period can feel difficult: the potential is there but it is never feeling fully achieved. If desired, to achieve the pivot from talent intelligence as a side-of-the-desk activity to a Talent Intelligence function, you need to be clear and decisive and it needs a hard reset of the organization. This is not to say the activities previously undertaken were not worthwhile or valuable but, much like if you were starting from a clean slate or greenfield environment, it is important to take this time to ensure that you have the vision in place, you understand your customer base appropriately (rather than just inheriting the previous customer base) and you understand what resources are needed to take you through this journey. Let's look into this more.

Who, why, how and what?

Whenever you are looking to create either a talent intelligence capability or a Talent Intelligence function, I would always start off by really clarifying what you want to achieve. Be clear about your vision, your mission, what should be your remit and, most importantly, who your customer is. Then, equally, reflect and be clear about what is out of scope and what is beyond your remit.

Who is your customer?

This is arguably the single most important question any person will face when setting up a talent intelligence capability. On the face of it, this usually seems to be a very easy question to answer, but it often gets more nuanced and more difficult to answer. This is especially the case when you question whether someone is a customer or a stakeholder. Remember, anyone who decides they are a stakeholder is one. Customers, on the other hand, are those whose needs you are trying to satisfy through building this capability.

The best way to determine who is your customer is to think about what you want to achieve and what impact you want to have as a function. Why do you even think this capability is needed within your organization? Where is the need? Some of this will come from the red flags and pain points (to be discussed later). Be really clear about what are you trying to achieve by having this capability existing. Do not do this process in isolation – go and talk to stakeholders. At this stage, it can be hard to quantify who is/isn't a stakeholder, but equally often that means there are very few barriers. Go and talk to talent acquisition leaders, marketing leaders, sales leaders, market leaders; really try and understand their pain. What is making their lives difficult? Where are they trying to drive to and what will stop them getting there?

More often than not, the issue of people, or lack thereof, is cited as the primary factor in both current difficulties and risk for future growth or developments. This is a clear buying signal, i.e. this is a sign that they are interested in what you are suggesting/selling and that they could be a core customer. Therefore, talent acquisition functions are often seen as the main customer for talent intelligence teams or individuals. Teams and individuals then sit organizationally and this is where this function gets created. Talent acquisition could be the main customer but I would argue often they are the main recipient for SI (sourcing intelligence); subsequently, they are the vehicle to the customer for talent intelligence.

Let's reflect on the definition we are using for Talent Intelligence:

> Talent Intelligence is the augmentation of internal and external people data with the application of technology, science, insights and intelligence relating to people, skills, jobs, functions, competitors and geographies to drive business decisions.

The key phrase here is *to drive business decisions*. Be clear about whether your customers are in fact the drivers of those business decisions or if they are they simply informing those decision makers. If they are simply informing those decision makers – and are not the decision makers themselves – then I would argue that you have the wrong customer base and you should be focusing on the end customer.

Does your route to market really matter?

This may sound like semantics, after all, as long as the intelligence reaches the right person does the route to market even matter? I would argue that it does and the reason is simple: key performance indicators (KPIs). A KPI is a measurable value that demonstrates how effectively a person/team/organization/business is achieving key objectives. Every goal/KPI at any individual level should have a clear line of sight through the team goals/KPIs, the functional goal/KPIs and to the business goals/KPIs. It is well established that KPIs will drive behaviours. If you are in a function whose KPIs and goals are at odds with creating the type of talent intelligence delivery that the end customer needs, then it is virtually impossible to build an effective and stable talent intelligence organization.

What does an example of this look like? Well, say you are a Talent Intelligence analyst tied to talent acquisition and a recruiter is struggling to hire in a given location. Your traditional internal customer problem statement may read something like the following:

> We are looking to expand our software function by XX headcount over the next 12 months in this location. We are currently struggling to resource up in an effective manner and this is leading to increased time to hire and putting pressure on delivery for the business. We need to complete a review of the total addressable market, review the competitors and their offerings and a salary review. A successful outcome will enable us to achieve this year's headcount growth on time and in budget without needing external agency support. The measures of success will be YY number of placements impacted by talent intelligence research and a reduction of time to hire by ZZ days.

They may engage with you to do salary benchmarking, a competitor analysis, an organizational design benchmarking, look at the total addressable market, etc. All of this is valuable and interesting work, intended to impact the design of the customer team and improve the likelihood of a fast and effective placement (likely their KPIs would be tied around time to hire, cost of hire, etc.). On the face of it, this would be a successful project perfectly aligned with the KPIs of that team; albeit it might be hard to track or measure, but we will cover that later.

Now look at the same problem statement if we take it from the end decision maker's stance, whose KPIs are built around the overall business health and business customer commitments:

> We are looking to expand our software function by XX headcount over the next 12 months in this location. We are currently struggling to resource up in an effective manner and this is leading to increased time to hire, resulting in missed customer commitments, exposing us to £XXm in fines and putting at risk our broader five-year engagement plan with the customer and the associated £XXm contract renewal. We need to assess

mitigation strategies at both this site, but also review future feasibility of this location and what other locations or remote-working options are feasible within this time zone to make sure we have the right people in the right place to ensure stability and sustainability for the function. The measures of success will be: a successful five-year development plan, to see what headwinds we will face, what challenges we can expect, how the labour market is shifting and then to recommend solutions and strategies to combat these challenges, enabling us to have growth and stability without missing any customer timeline commitments.

As we can see, although on the face of it these were similar problem statements the overall need and KPIs drive a very different outcome of project need in terms of level of work, type of data and strategic mindset.

This shifting mindset of operational to strategic is critical and one of the reasons why it is so vital to be really clear about who the customer is both in terms of organization/business unit/market and level, in order to ensure you are engaging with the decision makers. This will not only enable you to design and build a more appropriate Talent Intelligence function for your business, but also reduce wasted resource.

It is useful to think of a customer and talent intelligence workflow as being somewhat similar to oil production, with upstream and downstream: upstream being where the decisions are being made; downstream where these decisions are landing operationally in the business. Often, if research is at the end point downstream from a decision, it cannot affect any outcomes, so you will end up spending a huge amount of time, energy and resources to purely mitigate the effects of a poor upstream decision. It is far more effective to go as far upstream in the decision-making process as possible to be able to influence that decision, rather than dealing with the outcome/symptoms of poor decisions downstream later.

Vision, mission and principles

WHY ARE YOU DRIVING TOWARDS THIS: YOUR VISION?

When you are thinking of your vision and mission: think big. The vision statement should be the strategic view of what you want to build towards in the future. This is the overall purpose of the function and the output. Why do you exist?

This could be something such as:

> The Global Talent Intelligence team will enable and empower our leadership with the right market data, analysis and intelligence, at the right time to drive impactful strategic decisions.

I would highly recommend not creating a team vision in isolation. Use a workshop or meeting to bring together team members, or your broader stakeholder depending on team size, and have an open forum with facilitation. Look to start with a guiding statement or vision that the group can broadly agree on. This should be ambitious yet realistic; it should align with the company's goals and be attainable and achievable for your team or function. This is really the time to get everyone in the meeting involved. Get them to really thrash out ideas, concepts and mechanisms to make sure that what you are setting as a vision is aligned to their own personal goals but also to give them a sense of responsibility and ownership over the vision, and associated success, of your Talent Intelligence function.

Most importantly, once solidified and agreed upon, do not let this vision sit in the proverbial desk draw gathering dust. Use it: make it visible; have it front and centre of your work as your reminder and your north star to aim at. This is what you strive to achieve, what you want to drive towards, so make it a regular part of your communications verbiage.

HOW ARE YOU DRIVING TOWARDS IT: YOUR MISSION?
The mission is more around the operational mechanisms in place to get you there in the present. Both vision and mission are vital and can be core to setting up what you want to be and how you want to get there.

The mission could be presented like this:

> Delivery of talent intelligence work will be made to the end customer and decision maker. We will look to leverage existing relationships with the business via partner teams and inject talent intelligence into the relevant process mechanisms to ensure appropriate access and delivery.

WHAT DO YOU STAND FOR: YOUR PRINCIPLES?
I would also recommend setting up some core principles of what you are. You will often hear people talk about core principles or tenets. Within this setting they can be vital to help guide and steer the team on day-to-day decisions and direction. These will be the foundations that will set the tone for your work and the teams' ethos and culture.

Examples of potential talent intelligence tenets could be:

- We make recommendations based on research and evangelize data-driven decision-making.
- We identify and solve the root cause of problems rather than their symptoms.
- We prioritize work that results in measurable impact for our customers.
- We provide self-service and custom talent intelligence solutions to our customers globally.

Pain points, red flags and anomalies

Traditionally, the first steps in creating a talent intelligence capability are to either look for the pain points, the red flags happening within your organization, or to look towards the strategy and growth plans and what can limit the ability to achieve this. Usually, talent intelligence teams are created from within talent acquisition or executive recruitment, so we will initially look at the potential pain points, red flags and anomalies that you may see from within here.

Often the initial red flags can be uncovered through analysing data, whether from HR analytics or talent acquisition analytics, but equally these can be anecdotally understood through talking to your customer/stakeholder group. But what could these pain points look like?

Initial pain points, red flags and anomalies could include:

- locations with abnormally high time to hire
- locations with high attrition rates
- roles with high agency spend versus similar roles in other locations
- teams with higher-than-average attrition rates
- roles with higher-than-average time to hire
- roles where misalignment between allocated role salary budget versus that of external market realities
- roles/markets where you know competitors are ramping up hiring
- roles with unusually high demand forecast by the business

Of course, not everything is a red flag. There can be 'green flags' that have a risk of turning amber or red if they are not achieved.

- Your time to hire could be looking strong and in the green, but month-on-month you start to see it extending out into the amber range. This could be a potential flag to look into to see the context. What has changed? What is the external context? What is the market condition?

- Your attrition rate could be well within normal parameters but you see the warning signs of it starting to slip. Once again, what has changed? How has employee engagement moved? What is the external sentiment analysis showing? What about competitor talent flows? Have you had any leaders leave who are acting as talent magnets?

- You see your offer decline rate is rapidly increasing and you are having to work much harder in recruitment channel efforts to make the same number of hires. What is the context? Do your candidates have multiple offers? Are they being counter-offered? Is the recruiter requisition volume at the same level? Has the market moved on from a compensation perspective and you are no longer competitive?

- You see your candidate application rates are dropping month-on-month and this is putting your growth/hiring plans at risk. What is the candidate perception if you look at external sentiment? Has your job advert copy changed? Are there new competitors in your market/job segment? What is happening with your corporate brand in the marketplace?

Fundamentally, though you are looking for abnormalities, you are looking for changes (whether current or forecast), for instability, for problems or potential problems. Do not focus on the normal activity. Focus on the outliers (positive or negative) and dig into the potential impact of these outliers. This is a fantastic chance to get proactive and start looking round corners for your business.

Loss leader projects

When you are first building a team/capability, I would always recommend looking to create a series of loss leader projects. This name comes from retail and is a pricing strategy where a product or service is sold at a price below its market cost to stimulate other sales of more profitable goods or services. Although it does not translate directly to the world of TI, in my mind the name serves the purpose. These are projects where there is no defined customer or pre-defined red flag or pain point, but it is an area where you can see the pain coming down the road and you're being proactive. You may not have a defined return on investment, and leaders at your organization may not have even expressed an interest in the topic area, but if it is an area you are passionate about and see the potential impact being important enough, then this is what you are looking for. The reason for doing this work is twofold:

1 for it to act as a catalyst for change and to spark conversations internally on the topic area. It may not give all the solutions but should prompt a conversation

2 it is a marketing tool for you as a talent intelligence function. It is allowing you to get work to a level in the organization and a breadth across the organization that your traditional work wouldn't necessarily allow yet

But what could these loss leaders look like? These are topics that are usually leadership level. Management or leadership will not necessarily be aware of the topic area that needs to be addressed, but they are usually business critical topics such as:

- the macro effect of remote working on the organization
- looking at demographical forces and their impact on the company, such as with retirement cliffs, candidate pipeline issues or knowledge transfer with the retirement of baby boomers
- the impact of a specific geopolitical decision on your talent pipeline (such as wars or visa regulation changes)
- industry-level pipeline problems that are not being addressed (think along the lines of the 2021/2022 truck driver shortage – this was forecast out for 10 years by industry analysts, but very few firms actually had robust plans in place as to how to deal with this)
- executive level diversity or attrition rates at a macro level

If you are wanting to be more targeted it could be:

- the effect of a talent competitor entering your market/geography
- a macro analysis of candidate sentiment for your organization
- a competitor launching a new product range or pivoting, bringing in a new leadership team, changing their complete philosophy and looking at how that could affect you as an organization

These projects are, by their nature, unlikely to give an answer (as you do not necessarily have a question in mind), but they will open up discussion and show your function's capabilities.

Building use cases and products

So, you have identified your customers, nailed the vision, mission and team principles; you have had stakeholder meetings and have a long list of pain points and potential red flag projects – now what?

First, take a step back.

Remember that you cannot try to solve all the, identified problems at the same time.

If you are reading this, then you are likely looking to bring talent intelligence to an organization that does not already have it. This means that there is a big education piece needed to inform stakeholders of what Talent Intelligence is, how long it takes and what to expect. This education is vital in terms of setting realistic expectations and setting yourself up for success, especially in the early days of the function. It is understandable – you have found all these problems and you want to try and solve them all. You want to build trust and credibility with the customers by delivering and you want to prove the value of Talent Intelligence immediately. But just take a step back. Look to give all projects a score to give you a prioritization list (jump to Chapter 5 to find out more about this), look at the low-hanging fruit, the quick wins and look at what is going to give you the relevant trust building projects with the key customers.

As a side note, one element I often see is individuals looking to set up strategic Talent Intelligence functions naturally heading back towards talent acquisition and sourcing intelligence. This is absolutely normal. It is a safer space so if you're having a crisis of confidence, which happens to us all when we are setting things up, it is an easy space to slip back into. With a crisis in confidence, many question whether their intel is valid, robust enough and so on. This is a healthy paranoia but it is worth remembering that if you did not give your talent intelligence to customers, the business would still have to make a decision – it would just be without having any information at all to support it. Some intelligence, if even directional, is better than none; just be clear about what it is and what it is not.

So, you have your initial project list, have prioritized and know what you are going to attack. Now is the time to start thinking about what solutions you can offer to the earlier problems. What can you build out this year?

What will you lay foundationally for subsequent years? What needs to be true or happen in order to solve all the problems? What are projects (e.g. a one-off location decision) versus ongoing programmes of work (e.g. annual DEI feasibility or goal setting, always on marketing intelligence, etc.). You do not have to have all the answers, but you need to be clear about what you can achieve in the short/medium/long term and what is needed from an investment perspective to achieve the desired goals.

At this initial phase, I would recommend also framing projects as pilots rather than ongoing future commitments to work. This gives you the opportunity to experiment with product, customers and output and see if there is an appetite and projects and programmes are feasible, but this also gives you the breathing room to be able to say that to launch fully you need extra resource, etc. Let's dive into the resource side of things a little deeper.

Choosing resources

After identifying pain points and red flags and use cases, you are now starting to see what dedicated resources you will need. Think about what is available internally from a skill, product output and partner team perspective. These initial days are, by their very nature, very scrappy. As we will discuss later, at these stages you will often be a jack-of-all-trades but a master of none, but it is worth remembering the full quote is actually 'a jack-of-all-trades is a master of none, but oftentimes better than a master of one'. Know that it will be messy and you will feel stretched, but things will focus as you scale and mature.

Be clear on what is feasible from a resource perspective. Your capacity will be limited and demand will be high. Look at what partner teams you can align with – are there individuals in HR analytics, marketing intelligence or M&A already looking at some elements of talent intelligence? How can you align? Are there people in talent acquisition who have a passion for talent intelligence? Could they shadow and support on projects or come over on a rotation programme? Does your organization have an intern programme or a graduate programme that is centrally funded and could they rotate into your talent intelligence team to help build this out? On average, most researchers can carry 1.5 projects at a time and the average project duration is 30 to 40 days. This means that you have very limited bandwidth across an entire year. Be clear to leadership about this and show what the return on investment of effective talent intelligence is (jump into Chapter 6 for more information on metrics for success).

This is also the time to start thinking about team composition from head count and structure perspective, which could be analysts, project managers, economists, knowledge managers, etc. (covered further in Chapter 10) and also the tools and vendor partnerships (Chapter 9) that you will need in place to succeed.

Building trust

Whether your team deliver self-service products or consulting services, any output that is not bought into and used does not make return on investment. Without people buying into your solutions, your TI product and solutions will fail, so really think about how your products and services launch, how you build and gain buy-in and how you build trust with your customers.

Have a brand/branding

I am a firm believer that every talent intelligence team, be it a large team or an individual contributor, should have their own brand. It is their own identifying symbol, mark, logo, name, word, or sentence to distinguish their product and research from all others out there – internally and externally. This is integral to building your credibility, building your audience and, ultimately, building your reputation as a trusted resource. This branding is also vital in forming a sense of collective identity for your organization as your team grows. This can be vital as individuals within talent intelligence can often feel a little lost in their broader organizations before their true home is found, whether that is in talent acquisition, talent management, strategy or centralized intelligence (all to be discussed in Chapter 7).

Tell your story

Within this brand it is important to tell the story of your offering – how you came about, what you stand for, what you are going to build, etc. This will all shape how your customer base and audience perceive you and your output. This is another reason why it is so important to have a clear vision, mission and tenets/principles.

Be open, honest and transparent

There is no shortcut to gain customers' trust. You have to work for it and earn it. As with so much in business and life, being open, honest and transparent is a great starting point to help forge this trust. Be open about your journey, your product, your strengths and weaknesses as a function as well as your limitations. Be open, direct and transparent. If you drop the ball, which will happen at some point (we all have situations that arise), then be open and take ownership and responsibility for the situation. Your customers are on your side. The best outcome is one where you are all succeeding to drive the overall business goals forward. Having partners working with them who they know will be open and transparent with them is invaluable and this will help foster the trusted adviser relationship we are after.

Know your target audience

As mentioned earlier, understanding your customer is arguably the most important element in building out any talent intelligence capability. Core to this is understanding your target audience. This is as valid for delivering research and sending communications or for targeting talent intelligence partnering and team development opportunities internally. Spend time getting to know your customers. Understanding their key drivers, their pain and their needs will enable you to build out custom solutions for their specific needs – not only adding value to them but also demonstrating you understand them as a customer, central to building trust.

Good judgement/expertise

You will not always give customers what they want to see but you should give them what they need to see. When you are seen as a true talent intelligence strategic adviser it will be because not only are you well-informed and knowledgeable, understanding the technical aspects of the work as well as having a depth of experience, but you will also leverage this to challenge leaders and exercise good judgement. You will look to the future and not sacrifice the short-term decision or advice for the sake of the long-term relationship.

Put a face to the name

In today's remote, time-constricted world, meeting customers face to face or even virtually can be challenging. As a minimum I would recommend having a 'meet the team' page on either a wiki, or on the sign-off on any comms newsletter. This lets customers really get to know you as individuals beyond the brand. This is absolutely vital in the process of building trust.

Ask for and act on feedback.

Once you are working with clients, and hopefully delivering excellent work, never rest on your laurels. Constantly ask for feedback and look for areas for development (Chapter 5). This shows customers that you care. Most importantly, though, act upon the feedback you receive. This demonstrates that you are listening and that their voice is heard.

Barriers to entry

Rather controversially, I would suggest that by design you should look to potentially create barriers to entry from a project request perspective. This can be vital to reduce demand and increase capacity needed to drive the projects identified as high priority. Barriers to entry for project engagement could be: non-automated intake, levelling and project sponsor and defined measurable business impact value.

NON-AUTOMATED INTAKE

Although having an automated intake or online form intake makes the intake process in some ways much easier, as you will have a lot of the fields already populated, there are some dangers to be aware of:

- If this is your only intake mechanism (i.e. no follow-up call or meeting), then you are in danger of not having sufficient information to ensure a robust project plan.
- If this is part of your initial intake process in the customer's mind, that is the day you start working on their project. This immediately puts you on the back foot as when you do follow up for a further intake after five, ten or twenty days (or whatever your internal mechanism is), then the customer already feels like that is wasted time. This puts you under undue pressure to deliver and ultimately disappoints the customer.

LEVELLING AND PROJECT SPONSOR

To ensure that you are working on the right things, and to help manage capacity planning, it is advisable to require that leaders are aware of new projects requested. What that level of leader is will entirely depend upon your organization, but I would say from a levelling perspective they should sit at strategic road-mapping or decision-making level at a minimum. This will help you prioritize workload, articulate the business problem and/or the measurable impact and remove duplicative requests. Sponsors should be expected to join the intake and delivery meetings and have an active participation throughout the work.

MEASURABLE BUSINESS IMPACT VALUE

One area in which I have seen a lot of talent intelligence teams struggle is to articulate the value and impact of their work (see more in Chapter 6). What I would argue is that, by making this a prerequisite for project intake, you both save your own pain in articulation but also ensure that your customers have really thought through a problem *before* they reach out to you for support. This alone will reduce the 'nice to have' requests. You can also have pre-defined impact levels before you will work on projects. This could be any amount but the easiest way to gauge this value is to take your average time to completion, multiplied by a cost per day (your own cost or cost avoidance versus a research firm), multiplied by whatever multiplier of value you wish to have (10X is a common value to pick).

Now it is worth noting it can sometimes be very hard to articulate the measurable impact value on some projects. This does not mean you should not work these projects; just be conscious of what other project intake requirements are needed. The most common, if no measurable impact value can be articulated, are:

- projects being aligned to your own team goals (for example, customer expansion, up levelling of projects and so on)
- projects being aligned to larger strategic goals (such as DEI strategy, early careers strategy)

There will always be situations where a very senior leader will need support but their problem does not fit the criteria for the team's intake. If you can complete these it can be fruitful in terms of building trust and becoming a trusted adviser. Be clear, however, about your capabilities and what you should be used for as a team/individual.

There is a lot to digest in the above. Know this is not a sprint. You do not need to achieve all of the above immediately. Pick your battles and pace yourself.

Summary

This has been a busy chapter – there's a lot to draw together in this conclusion. Let's be very clear – building out a talent intelligence capability or Talent Intelligence function is hard. This is a new space, the vendor landscape (as we will discuss in Chapter 9) is still very complicated, the definitions are confusing, the customer base is ill-defined, the product output (to be discussed in Chapter 5) is wide-ranging, the problem statements will be blurry and customer identification is challenging… but any company in an industry that is changing, where they themselves are changing and where their talent competitors are changing, will have a need for talent intelligence.

The demand for your work, the pull factor, will not be a problem. Having enough supply of talent intelligence, the capacity management, will be the biggest issue and has been in every talent intelligence team I have spoken to throughout my time in this space. Once leaders see that they can finally have labour market intelligence at a granular level, there will be a tsunami of work. In fact, most teams I have spoken to have to actively control their communications and actively slow down their internal business development as they simply do not have resources to cover the breadth of the organization.

TOBY'S TAKEAWAYS

- Ensure people can articulate why they need your help rather than you trying to articulate why your work is of value to them.

- Have project sponsors in place to help with prioritization and to be your cheerleaders and advocates at a senior level.

- Always have your core projects (usually initially those identified as pain points and red flags), but equally think about the larger loss-leader projects.

- Create a brand: give it life and meaning so that it can stand for something.

- Create barriers to entry and control mechanisms to ensure you work on projects that are of real value not just 'nice to have'.

- Building trust is your number one priority throughout.

05

What type of work can TI functions support?

In this chapter, we are going to dig into the structuring and mechanism behind an effective intelligence process before diving into the types of projects and products that your talent intelligence capability could support. Now it is worth reiterating that both the mechanism and the types of projects you will look to support will be heavily dependent upon your organization, your customer base and the definition of Talent Intelligence you are leaning towards. But for now, we will dive into the mechanism of a talent intelligence project and what that would look like.

Structuring a talent intelligence process

The five phases of military intelligence collection are planning and preparation, approach, questioning, termination and reporting.[1] This is mirrored somewhat in a Talent Intelligence environment where we see: needs capture, planning, research, project delivery, post-project wash up and stakeholder feedback mechanism. Let's dive into each of these sections and look into what the structure of a talent intelligence process could be.

Needs capture

In this stage it is key to really understand the business/organization/customer business goals and problem statement. The mechanism on this can vary between organizations, from a formal intake meeting to an online form. But the purpose remains the same. The following questions can be a useful guide as you begin:

- What is the key issue you are trying to resolve?
- What is the measurable impact of this research and what are for success?
- What are the key data points needed to affect the decision poi
- What parameters are in/out of scope?
- Who are the key stakeholders that need to be informed through this process?
- What is the timescale needed for delivery?
- What is the confidentiality level of the project?

You could also look at gathering further data points such as the priority level of the project, the business area you are supporting, the type of project (e.g. location assessment, skills assessment, competitor analysis, M&A intelligence, candidate listening), the headcount needed to support projects... Who is the primary stakeholder and what is their corporate grade or level? Similarly, who is the project sponsor and their corporate grade or level? What is the business impact value of the work? How many headcounts will be impacted by this work and what is their average salary? How many locations are in scope for the work? All of these, and more, data points can be incredibly useful to capture in order to create a narrative with your management information. Are you supporting one business a disproportionate amount? Do you see regular repeat business from certain stakeholders? Do you see a big demand for certain project types by customer group? What is the overall business measurable impact value?

The simplest way to ensure you are capturing all you need in this session is to have a structured intake form to remind you of what is needed (please see an example at the end of this chapter).

Two areas you may have noted on the intake parameters were the project confidentiality level and the project prioritization. Before we jump into more detailed project planning, let's take a moment or two just to look into these to better understand what they look like.

CONFIDENTIALITY LEVEL

Within your work I would recommend creating a list of defined confidentiality levels. This is important to ensure data partitioning and data security.

There are two philosophies you can adopt with data confidentiality:

1 Restricted first

A restricted first philosophy to project confidentiality will assume that all projects are highly restricted by default and you will work with the stakeholders to open up projects and data sharing to the minimum amount needed for the project to be completed successfully. This would likely have a large number of non-disclosure agreements (NDAs) and be within a data restrictive environment.

2 Open first

The opposite of this is an open first philosophy where, as a default stance, projects are open to all and unrestricted. You then work with the customers and stakeholders to see how much you have to restrict the project to ensure all goals are met.

There is no right or wrong method or philosophy here, but it is important to be clear about what you are and the pros and cons of both.

Restricted first gives very good data and project control. Customers' and stakeholders' trust is built; they know your confidentiality is ensured and that project confidentiality is maintained. It does however create artificial siloes where data is usually restricted further than it needs to be and opportunities for knowledge sharing and partnering can be lost.

Open first is a fantastic way to break down siloes, knowledge share and look at pan-function, pan-business and pan-silo collaboration on projects and initiatives. However, it can mean, if they do not understand the philosophy fully, that customers are initially hesitant coming to you with the most sensitive topics for fear of general publication and a lack of data control.

Once you have a clear philosophy, think about what confidentiality level is appropriate for the project. Traditionally the four levels of information classification are:

- confidential (only senior management have access)
- restricted (most employees have access)
- internal (all employees have access)
- public information (everyone has access)

I would recommend partitioning this a little further and having something such as:

- confidential to project team
- confidential to talent intelligence
- confidential to leadership
- restricted to customer group (e.g. talent acquisition)
- internal access
- open access/unrestricted

You can then use this to set rules and data partitioning for any kind of knowledge management system, library system or communications plan you may put in place for the dissemination of information and knowledge management.

PRIORITIZATION MATRIX

A prioritization matrix is vital for effective workload management. This is usually a combined value of urgency and importance while factoring in measurable impact, level of stakeholder and organizational goal alignment.

Let's look at an example of what this could look like:

Definitions

- Important – are activities that have an outcome that leads to achieving goals related to Talent Intelligence functional strategic goals. These should be evaluated and defined after a project intake during a queue review.
- Urgent – are those related to activities that lead to achieving goals associated to project stakeholders defined as business value during the project intake. Be aware that just because something is high profile or has been escalated it does not necessarily mean it is automatically urgent.

Formula

Priority score – a project is given a score from 0 to 3 and designated a quadrant category based on the matrix below. This helps decide if we take on projects and determine the prioritization across projects.

Priority score = [Urgency Yes (1) + Urgency No (0)] + [Importance Yes (2) + Importance No (0)]

We can then use Eisenhower's Urgent/Important Principle (but written long form in this case for the book):

- Do this first: 3 points scored, High Importance, High Urgency
    - o These projects both fulfil strategic goals for the function and our customer. Typically, high visibility projects that have defined impact.
- Schedule: 2 points scored, High Importance, Low Urgency
    - o These projects fulfil the strategic goal of the function (such as customer expansion, sponsorship level) but maybe do not have clear business impact for the stakeholders involved.
- Delegate: 1 point scored, Low Importance, High Urgency
    - o These projects do not fulfil any strategic goals for the function but may have clear business impact given by the requestor. These may take the form of an 'ad hoc' or 'value add' type of project that allows us to gain the trust of a stakeholder.
- Do not do: 0 points, Low Importance, Low Urgency

Now this is only an example; your own prioritization matrix may want to factor in other elements: total number of hires impacted, business impact value, seniority of requestor, etc. or have a totally different scoring mechanism. Be clear to make sure the prioritization matrix model reflects the KPIs you want to drive as a team (Chapter 6) to ensure you are aligning work to the most impactful elements you are trying to achieve.

Planning and sign off

This phase is absolutely paramount to successful project completion. This is the stage where you will articulate what you are going to do, how you are going to get there and what the journey will look like. Within this phase you will look at the dependencies you may have:

- Are there internal or external teams you need to engage with for data?
- Do you have capacity to deliver the work needed?
- Do you have the skills needed to complete the work?
- Are the data sets you require available externally?
- Work backwards from the delivery date to see when you need to start which elements of the research.

This phase is often overlooked or rushed as teams and individuals look to get sign off and dive into the delivery mode, but it is important to spend the time at the front end to really ensure the project has maximum chance of success.

This is the stage to really look at all of the information gathered in the needs capture and to synthesize that down to have a clear and concise problem statement, to really understand the list of deliverables, delivery dates, what resources will be required and to articulate what the communications schedule will look like throughout the delivery phase post-project plan sign-off.

You can use this moment to tie down very specific project objectives using an alternative take on the SMART methodology:

- Specific – be very clear on the project objective and write this out in a crisp and concise manner that is easy for all to digest.

- Measurable – how do you know you have been successful on delivery of your project? Where possible use quantifiable language to ensure you know specifically what success will look like.

- Acceptable – is the project plan in line with what was captured in the needs capture and will it be accepted by the customer and sponsors?

- Realistic – is the project feasible? Are the objectives realistic to achieve? To ensure success, the objectives need to be realistic to achieve and attainable.

- Timebound – it can be very useful to have both the project and the objectives tied and timebound. This means having clean duration and completion dates and objectives should have a closure end date on them.

For example, a poor objective statement may be: 'We are struggling with our attrition; successful project outcome would be a project delivered that helps us reduce our attrition.'

Strengthening this up a little could make it: 'Attrition is rising by 5 per cent month on month and is currently sitting at 22 per cent, leaving us with a lost productivity of $300,000 per month. A successful project outcome would be a project delivered after five weeks that enabled us to action a specific lever to identify the core issues, reduce attrition to 15 per cent within the next business quarter.'

In this way, the project objective is clearly articulated and Specific, it is Measurable on the attrition rate, the delivery time and project goals are Acceptable, the goals of the project are Realistic with a project length and attrition target that are within reason, and the whole project and goal statement are Timebound.

Now we have a clear project plan in place, let's get that signed off with our customers.

PROJECT PLAN SIGN OFF

Once you have a clearly articulated plan in place, you should create a project plan, which is a one-page document highlighting everything captured up until this point. You should then send/review this with the customer for final sign off and approval. This is a vital catch point to both ensure all expectations are aligned and that the project has been captured and scoped out correctly. Within this you should reconfirm:

- problem statement
- deliverables
- success criteria
- in scope
- out of scope
- risks and interdependencies
- confidentiality level
- stakeholders
- project team
- timeline
- business articulated measurable impact/core strategic alignment

I would recommend never starting a project until this project plan has been confirmed and signed off. This is also vital in case things go wrong later in the project and, as part of a postmortem, you can review the project plan to confirm what was in scope, out of scope, expectations and deliverables, etc. Once this project plan has been signed off and agreed by all parties, we can get into the details and start the research.

Research

This is the stage when things get started in earnest. The research needed, the methods needed, the collation and the analysis will vary dramatically from study to study. Some will need aggregated macro labour market data; some will need primary research talking to candidates, recruiters, competitors to draw qualitative or quantitative data; you may need to review skills taxonomies; some will use OSINT and some HUMINT. This phase is as varied as the breadth of work that your team will take on. Throughout, though, it is vital to remain structured.

Have clear methodology; know how long each parameter may take to analyse and approach them in a logical order. Do not put off approaching data partners for data until the last minute when they may need days or weeks to deliver.

DATA CONFIDENCE MODEL

Now, when we are conducting our research, we will naturally gather a great deal of information from a huge variety of sources. With that in mind, one area that I think is going to grow in terms of importance as our access to data increases and as the field of Talent Intelligence matures is that of a data confidence model. This data confidence model is based on the UK Police Information report.[2]

Within this model you have three values: a Document Confidence Classification, a Data Source Classification and a Data Point Classification. Your Document Confidence Classification is the confidence value that you would place on the document as a whole. The Data Source Classification is the value you would place on the data source itself and then you will have a final Data Point Classification for the data point itself. This gives a holistic view of data validation and confidence from the individual data point right through to line of sight for the project as a whole.

Document Confidence Classification (DCC)

The Document Confidence Classification is broken down into three categories of confidence and rather simply these are High (H), Moderate (M) and Low (L) confidence levels. These are defined as follows:

- High confidence generally indicates judgements based on high-quality information, and/or the nature of the issue makes it possible to render a solid judgment. A 'high confidence' judgement is not a fact or a certainty, however, and still carries a risk of being wrong.

- Moderate confidence generally means credibly sourced and plausible information, but not of sufficient quality or corroboration to warrant a higher level of confidence.

- Low confidence generally means questionable or implausible information was used, the information is too fragmented or poorly corroborated to make solid analytic inferences or significant concerns or problems with sources existed.

As we can see, this document confidence classification is heavily based around the quality of the data itself. We then have a classification of the data sources themselves.

Data Source Classification (DSC)

In a similar vein to the DCC, the DSC is broken down into three confidence classification categories of Reliable (R), Untested (U) and Not Reliable (NR) defined as the following:

- Reliable – this grading is used when the source is believed to be both competent and information received is generally reliable. This may include information from human intelligence, technical, scientific and vendor sources. It is important that the two tests of competence and reliability/veracity are both met before a source is considered to be reliable. Where either test is not met, not reliable should be selected and the ground to doubt the reliability is specified.

- Untested – the source may not necessarily be unreliable, but the information provided should be treated with caution. Before acting on this information, corroboration should be considered. This would apply to information when the source cannot be determined.

- Not reliable – this should be used where there are reasonable grounds to doubt the reliability of the source. This may include concerns regarding the authenticity, trustworthiness, competence or motive of the source of data. Corroboration should be sought before acting on this information.

Then, finally, you have the data points themselves – scored from 1 to 5 as follows:

1 Known directly to the source – refers to information obtained first-hand. Care must be taken to differentiate between what a source experienced themselves and what a source has been told or heard from a third party.

2 Known indirectly to the source but corroborated – refers to information that the source has not witnessed themselves, but the reliability of the information can be verified by separate information that carries the

information/intelligence of assessment of 1. This corroboration could come from technical sources, other intelligence, investigations or enquiries. Care should be taken when ascertaining corroboration to ensure that the information that is presented as corroboration is independent and not from the same original source.

3 Known indirectly to the source – applies to information that the source has been told by someone else. The source does not have first-hand knowledge of the information as they did not witness it themselves.

4 Not known – applies where there is no means of assessing the information.

5 Suspected to be false – regardless of how the source came upon this information, there is a reason to believe the information provided is false.

So, with this, any given document or project would have an overall confidence rating (H, M or L), each data source used within the project will have a confidence score (R, U, NR) and the data points themselves will have a confidence score (1–5). This level of data interrogation is far greater than anything we currently see within talent intelligence, but I believe would be highly valuable to further improve the professionalism and credibility of the data sources we use and the trust and credibility of our function to business leaders.

Project delivery

So, you have the project signed off, you know your data sources and their confidence level; now it is time to pull this together into a project to deliver. Be clear about who will be using your research, how your work will be digested and what the appropriate mechanism for this will be.

It may be an open discussion with an Excel tool, modelling out various scenarios. It may be a white paper sent out as a widely dispersed piece of communications. It may be a targeted report that needs a pre-read before a full meeting and breakdown or it may be a presentation in PowerPoint, walking stakeholders through the research and the journey.

Whatever the mechanism and stakeholder group, be very clear about your objectives from the delivery mechanism. If you want tight control and feedback, then a broad communications white paper will not be appropriate. If you want to control the flow and the story of the data, then that will be very hard to do on a pre-read and follow-up meeting.

Post-project wash up

Within teams this is arguably the most important step and one that is often overlooked. This is the internal wash-up session where everyone from the talent intelligence team that was involved in a project takes a step back, a moment to pause, reflect and think about how the project was delivered.

A wash-up meeting takes place at the end of a project and its purpose is to review the project as a whole, to review how successful the project was and if there are any improvements or updates to processes that need to be made. The wash-up is the final part of the project delivery process before the team moves onto the next project.

It is fully understandable how this gets missed; teams are usually so busy in delivery mode with a pipeline of work waiting for them. Carving out time and headspace for a project review is often simply not on their radar or high on the prioritization list. However, whether done face to face or virtually, I would argue that this session should be *the* most important and highest priority on any workload list.

This is the moment to review what went well, what could have gone better and what can be improved for next time. This is the moment to go over the intake, review the delivery, analyse the output and really take a holistic helicopter view. Did we really do all we could do to deliver the best output for our customer? If not, then why not?

RULES FOR THE WASH UP

There are a few important rules to follow for these sessions:

- This is about learning – this is *not* a time to assign blame for any failings or poor work, but rather this is the time to mitigate those situations from happening again in the future.
- This is a stage for reflection, growth and development and is a safe space to talk with no judgement.
- There is no hierarchy – this is an open and equal forum, no matter who is in attendance or who is facilitating.
- It is important to remain objective, step back from your own personal views and focus purely on the project's process and success.

To ensure these meetings run well, I would recommend having a somewhat standardized agenda. This not only gives the meeting structure but also allows the team member(s) to think ahead of time about what they want to bring up and discuss.

Think about a basic agenda framework such as:

- Did we achieve the goal set out in the intake document?
- What did we do well?
- What went wrong?
- If we did this project again, what would we do differently?

It is also worth considering having the full project process broken down into the various stages and swim lanes of stakeholders or partner teams responsible and ask team members to rate each stage of the process on how happy/engaged they were at that stage or how effectively they felt that stage worked overall, etc. This can be done on a score (1–5 or 1–10), a RAG status (red for poor, amber for needs improvement, green for strong), or a simple happy or sad face placed throughout the timeline. This is a very quick and effective way to see pain points in the process for both individual team members and partner teams as well as the project as a whole.

With follow-through questions such as:

- How could communication have been clearer?
- How could deadlines have been met?
- What were the reasons for bottlenecks in capacity?
- How could expectations have been set differently?

And most importantly

- What do we need to do to avoid making the same mistake(s) going forward?
- What lessons have we learnt?

At the end of any wash-up session, it is important to ensure things are fully captured and that there are clear learnings but, most importantly, that action plans and improvements to ensure these lessons learnt are embedded in future work. This can be in a structured form, a survey or it could be a shared 'washup log' – as long as it is clear, structured and accessible.

I would recommend periodically auditing these feedback notes to see if there are recurrent themes and to see if lessons truly are being learnt or whether the same issues are arising time and time again. This is important not just for the immediate project team but also for wider organizational, partner teams and stakeholder learning, development and evolution.

Stakeholder feedback mechanism

This is the single most valuable stage of any project from a customer development and trust perspective. The mechanism for taking stakeholder feedback can vary: some will choose an online form or survey, others an in-person feedback session. The key thing to ensure a valuable and enriching feedback session is to be clear about the goals of the session:

- This is for development and review. This is not a mechanism to capture feedback to score and rate individuals against (as that may create a bias in the feedback given).
- The aim is to walk away with clear qualitative and quantitative data points around the piece of work delivered and how you can improve as a team/function/output.
- This is a reinforcement meeting to also continue to build your relationships with key stakeholders.

Typical example questions to ask in a feedback session would be:

- Net Promoter Score (NPS): how likely are you to recommend Talent Intelligence to a colleague?
- Customer Satisfaction (CSAT): how satisfied are you with our product/ services?
- Customer Effort Score (CES): how easy did we make it for you to solve your issue?
- How would you rate the timeliness of delivery?
- How would you rate the communication of the team?
- How would you rate the accuracy of the research provided?
- How valuable has this research been to your decision-making process?
- What is the main reason for your scores?
- What could we do better?

Personally, I have always preferred doing these sessions face to face or virtually rather than an online form. One of the main reasons for this is to have a strong completion rate. Online forms traditionally have a very low completion rate and, when you are dealing with low volume and high value projects such as those in Talent Intelligence, this mechanism would not give enough data points for any meaningful feedback. The second reason I like to take these calls 'in person' is that we can use this time to influence the business and its leadership far more strategically than we may have done if not. We can really see how research is landing and how it is impacting. If things are not going according to plan, this can be a time for reputation management or expectations alignment. This can also be a fantastic opportunity to business develop for the function as it is an opportunity to see what else is coming in the pipeline that Talent Intelligence could support with and to find out what the issues are that are keeping your customer up at night which you could look to solve, etc. This is vital for team development, product development and to build trust with your customer base. These exploratory conversational opportunities would be missed if feedback was taken via a survey or form.

What are the types of projects to get involved with?

This is a somewhat loaded question as it really does depend on the definition of talent intelligence you are using and the partner or support teams already in place. For the purpose of this section, I will use a broader view of Talent Intelligence to also include talent acquisition analytics (but notably not TA efficiency reporting) and sourcing intelligence, but we will not be exploring the extended world of HR analytics or people analytics.

Talent acquisition analytics and sourcing intelligence

Talent acquisition analytics (TAA) and sourcing intelligence (SI) are the most common starting points for most Talent Intelligence functions and, at the point of writing this, where most of the broader definition talent intelligence activity is still situated.

Within TAA and SI you can dive into such topics as pipeline analysis, application channel analysis, looking to reduce time to hire, cost per hire, etc.

Market mapping

Market mapping, also sometimes referred to as total addressable market as mapping (see box), is as much an art as it is a science. It is a way of using competitive intelligence to understand how many candidates are in the market, who employs most of them, what the demand (job) and supply (candidate) ratio is, what the average salary in market is, DEI data about the market, etc. – and then using all the information to identify the best approach for your sourcing plan. It provides the business and talent acquisition with the analysis and insights of a market, especially competitors, and the employment status of high-quality passive talents who work in it. This all aids in setting the hiring feasibility, highlighting potential challenges in the search criteria which can help ensure your business is better prepared for attracting the best candidates at the right level, location and diversity ratio.

TOTAL ADDRESSABLE MARKET MAPPING

I would argue that this term, although popular, is often misunderstood and misused. More often than not, what people actually produce are insights into the Total Accessible Market, not the Total Addressable Market. The former being the available talent around which they have visibility, and often access to, and the latter being the actual total market that is out there. This variation is often due to a combination of platform market penetration and candidate behaviours around where they virtually exist.

Profile calibration

Sometimes tied into market mapping, but available as a separate offering, is profile calibration. This is a deeper dive into the profile itself and the role design, skills needed, basic qualifications needed, levelling of role, remit of role, etc. versus the rest of the competitor market to see if there is a fundamental misalignment of the role. This can then be used to springboard into a full market map, but this is not necessarily the case.

Sourcing playbook

Building out a sourcing playbook can be a fantastic way to both reduce duplicative requests but also provide actionable intelligence to recruiting and sourcing teams at scale. A playbook can be created to avoid recruiters starting a new search for existing markets, job functions or business lanes. The playbook helps talent acquisition to take a more targeted sourcing approach offering, and in return a reduced hiring cycle. What to include in

a playbook? Usually you would look at heavy effort but repe
outputs such as Boolean string generation, where you are look
often long, but usually standardized, search strings using B
(AND, OR, NOT, (), "", *, etc.). These would usually be ᴜ
against job titles, skills or parameters for diversity. So, for example, it wᴄ
were looking for a Talent Intelligence professional, a simple search string
could be:

(Talent OR Market) AND (insights OR intelligence OR analytics) within
a job title parameter AND "talent intelligence" as a skill.

This would find individuals with job titles such as talent insights, market
insights, talent intelligence, market intelligence, talent analytics, market
analytics that have also highlighted 'talent intelligence' as a skill.

Whether you are cutting by market, function or business lane, you can
create specific Boolean strings that can be used across the organization and
recruiters will not have to start from scratch each time. This could be a
string highlighting key competitors, specific skills, country-specific (language)
variations, DEI search parameters, university search parameters, etc. You
can of course look to optimize these Boolean strings for LinkedIn, Google
X-ray Search and social media with targeted platforms for different job
families, role function and location.

Historical candidate resurrection

This is an area of talent acquisition analytics that is often overlooked within
organizations due to frustrations with data analysis from their applicant
tracking systems (ATS). It is also not a traditional reporting mechanism but
can be incredibly valuable. Within this service you are cutting back into
historical candidate pools to unearth candidates who had previously been
live in a process but things had gone awry. This could be because the role
was closed down; it could be that recruiters left the organization and the
requisition fell between the gaps; it could be that someone else was hired
into the role and this person was a silver medallist... Whatever the reason,
there is often a trove of candidates who have already expressed an interest
in your organization and have likely already been interviewed to some
degree waiting to be resurrected. Whether your talent intelligence team
completes the outreach to resurrect, or whether they simply unearth and
highlight the missed opportunities and hand off to recruitment marketing,
sourcing or recruitment to re-engage is entirely dependent upon your model
and remits, etc.

Field alerts

This is a part of talent intelligence that ties very tightly into communications. Having a rapid response to activity in the market, such as lay-offs, mergers and acquisitions, start-up burn rates, executive movement/departures and competitor vulnerabilities, is vital in today's rapidly moving and changing talent landscape. Building a mechanism for these field alerts can be difficult: perhaps scraping at scale and having a network of data gatherers in market (usually in the form of recruiters), utililizing news alerts, etc. but also collating, processing and then pushing out the communications, whether by email, a regular updated wiki page, etc. It can be hugely valuable but the effort to build and maintain should not be underestimated.

Talent intelligence consulting

Talent intelligence consulting partners with the customer to allow the organization to scale and respond in an agile manner while mitigating risk and assessing feasibility from a labour market perspective. The purpose of this capability is to affect upstream business decisions using labour market intelligence to foster better decision-making and as a by-product have a positive downstream effect on teams such as talent acquisition.

Location strategy

Deep dive studies on global talent markets are needed to support team placement or expansion, including analysis of talent supply and demand, cost, risk, existing company presence and feasibility to sustain future growth. For all location work, it is important to understand who the key decision makers are and what the decision-making mechanism is. In most firms it will be real estate and you can look to partner with real estate teams to transform your physical footprint.

This is especially relevant given that the future of the workforce could look more distributed due to the increase in remote work. It is important to note though that these decisions are not always driven by real estate. It could be functional leaders looking at how to expand their organizations; it could be strategic workforce planning or it could be business leaders. Understand that these decisions are multi-faceted and that a strong stakeholder network will be needed.

You will likely want to pull upon finance and see any financial implications for tax relief there may be in given locations. HR or legal may want to get involved in looking at the ease of doing business. Public policy may want to be involved in terms of how you land in a given market, etc. We are not completing any of this work in isolation, so it is important to involve partner teams as much as possible as early as possible in the processes.

Talent flow analysis and skills-based intelligence

Adjusting talent acquisition and corporate strategies by understanding the movement of talent across employers, industries, geographies and identifying shifts in skills is vital. We can use this talent flow information to see which organizations are talent magnets, how they are expanding, how successful they are at targeting your top performers, if they are expanding equally in all markets or if they are targeting individuals in a new area that they haven't previously – suggesting a new venture. Equally, use this to prompt further reviews: are they a magnet due to higher compensation? Stronger candidate sentiment? Specific leadership being talent magnets? Is their organization design more conducive for the type of work candidates want? Are they more open to remote work? Do they have a stronger on-site culture?

You will rarely answer any questions via talent flows, but it will allow you to ask more powerful questions, especially when tracked and monitored over a time period.

M&A intelligence

It is widely accepted that an organization is only as good as its people. This is highlighted most within any M&A process. Any activity can give an opportunity to upgrade talent across the organization; in acqui-hire strategies, gaining access to highly-skilled employees is the primary reason for an acquisition. In early stage, pre-due diligence work, Talent Intelligence can work with M&A to really understand a given market. This is an early stage in the M&A process where the two parties will not be in contact. This is a chance to use talent intelligence's OSINT capabilities, really unpicking corporate structures and competitor intelligence. Talent intelligence can highlight potential M&A targets from a skills/talent perspective; they can review complementary footprints, go to market strategies, complementary corporate structures and complementary organizational cultures They can highlight any potential risks, be it retention issues, reputational issues, leadership challenges, etc. This is a facet that is largely missed currently in the early stage pre-due diligence process and can be hugely valuable to the M&A teams within organizations. Equally, through any M&A due diligence process there are times to review and to optimize workforce distribution, workforce levelling, geographic coverage, salary levelling, etc. These are all activities that talent intelligence can drive. Be open-minded and listen to your M&A teams to understand the key drivers behind the acquisition as that will drive the type of support and output they will need.

Cultural intelligence

Closely tied to M&A intelligence is a newly emergent field of cultural intelligence. Leila Mortet of Philips launched this element for them, serving as internal psychological research scientist, leading and supporting a variety of projects such as:

- development and implementation of scientific leadership and culture assessment for M&A target companies
- qualitative and quantitative human capital risk assessment for M&A targets
- talent assessments of potential M&A targets
- development of an agility-assessment and deriving strategic change management initiatives

This concept of using cultural intelligence and psychology as a lens to assess potential success or risk exposure lends itself to elements far outside of M&A activity. If you are launching into a new country, is that country culture likely to lend itself to your organization's working culture? If you are looking to launch a new team working style with distributed teams and fluid organizational structures, how will that work given the cultural norms in place already?

But this is not as far stretched and removed from your day-to-day as you may think. Psychology has and is being used extensively throughout the talent arena already:

- In talent assessment we have had various psychometric assessments for the last 20 years.
- In sourcing/talent acquisition we have had text analysis to assess gendered and diverse/non-diverse language choice, based on a number of psychology studies in the 1970s, for the best part of a decade.

- In recruitment marketing there has been an increasing int of behavioural science in advertising and marketing.

We are still working out what the space is in taler. behavioural and organizational psychologists but there certai... place for them.

Benchmarking analysis

Benchmarking can sometimes be a catch-all for various different products or outputs, but it is important to highlight. The key differentiator here is that you want to understand how your company compares to the external market – including, but not limited to, diversity representation, talent movement, talent management, sentiment analysis, organizational design, etc. Note the highlight on how your company compares. For true benchmarking analysis to occur, you will need as much internal data as possible. You will be tying in with HR analytics, compensation and benefits, organizational design, finance and real estate to name a few. True benchmarking is very hard. It takes a lot of time, effort and resource to really understand a competitor and match across to your own organization. I would always recommend to include as much primary research as possible. Talk to recent hires from those competitors and talk to recent leavers of the organization (ensure you know your own legal frameworks before doing this). You can find vast swathes of secondary and directional data online but talking to individuals will always unearth some contextual gold.

Diversity intelligence

By now there is a mountain of evidence to show why diversity across organizations is absolutely vital. To achieve this diversity without changing the status quo, without challenging traditional sourcing, recruitment, assessment, promotion, performance management or organizational design methodologies is nigh on impossible. We must do things differently; we must do things better. This might be:

- looking at non-traditional hiring pools, challenging historical hiring profile criteria (schools, degree requirements or previous employers)
- looking at funnel conversion metrics to see where there are bottlenecks in process from a DEI stance

looking at DEI feasibility across given job types/markets/business units and seeing areas for improvements versus market or competitor benchmarks

Diversity is one of the most challenging areas for any team, especially in geographies where government collected data is not as granular. There is a real lack of diversity data points at a granular level across nearly all roles, functions, industries and geographies outside of the United States. Be very clear about what you want to achieve with your diversity intelligence and data sets and what you are comfortable with from a data ethics perspective. For example, you may be struggling for diversity data for a certain job in a European country. You could theoretically scrape the social profiles of the people highlighted from the job parameters and use text analysis to look at their names and infer a gender; you could scrape the text in the profile to see schools or affiliations to strengthen this inference; or you could scrape their photos and infer an ethnicity. But this does not mean that this work is appropriate, just or ethical. Be very careful how you approach such topics and ensure your actions are ethical and in line with your relevant legislation at all times.

Candidate listening

Candidate listening/candidate perception is a mixed-methods research area to help us provide primary and secondary research on the talent market and execute upon our employer value proposition to attract the world's best talent. This also allows us to tie into: industry benchmarking, online reputation, areas of improvement and competitive intelligence.

This can be a macro analysis looking at large sets of candidate sentiment data such as feedback through the interview process. It can be looking at macro external data sets (Indeed, Glassdoor, Blind, etc.) that will show both what candidates are thinking about your process, but also what they are reading about you as an employer. It could also be more holistic social listening, looking at TikTok, Twitter, Facebook and so on. Although it can be harder to filter out the corporate brand versus talent brand. It is also vital to overlay this with primary research. Deep dive into specific talent populations, whether through interviews, surveys or focus groups, as it is vital to understand the key drivers of your talent population and how you are perceived by them.

Future intelligence: horizons and interventions

Arguably no other intelligence function has the ability to look into a crystal ball and predict the future of competitors in the same way as Talent Intelligence. It means you can look to the future 18 months plus (i.e. out to the future horizons) and see what headwinds you will face, what challenges to expect, how the labour market is shifting and then recommend solutions and strategies to combat these challenges (interventions).

This intelligence has become more popular at the macro level, with organizations hiring teams of economists to look at how the changing world is going to impact them as a business, but very few are taking the next step to look at how the changing world will affect them from a talent perspective. We have seen the outcomes of this already play out in real time. In the UK, we had the labour shortage due to Brexit; there is a global truck driver shortage even though the industry had been highlighting the issues for over a decade. Where will there be future talent shortages and talent gaps? Building a future intelligence – horizons and interventions offering (and arguably a sub function) composed of skilled business analysts and economists can help to alleviate this.

Battlecards

Battlecards, sometimes referred to as 'competitor comparisons' or 'competitor abstracts', are a visual aid that sales teams have historically used to provide a quick reference point to see how competitors stack up and compare around specific areas of interest, whether these are product specs, services, features, pricing, market penetration, etc. Salespeople use these to try to aid in convincing potential clients about the benefits of their value proposition while subtly highlighting potential weaknesses or flaws in competitor offerings.

In recent years, the battlecard concept has found a natural home in the recruitment community as the battle for talent has continued to intensify. Battlecards can be an efficient method of comparing strengths and weaknesses of your company, usually to a direct competitor but more recently with the increase in transitional skills, a talent competitor. There are two main methods for battlecard creation: primary and secondary data points. Most organizations will do these in reverse order. They will start with the secondary sources to gather as much scaled intelligence as possible, typically looking at: attrition rates, employee value proposition information, sentiment scores (career progression, leadership ratings, etc.), hiring patterns, their position on hot topics such as DEI or remote working, any kind of performance or compensation information such as review period, ratings or vesting schedule.

You can then augment this initial battlecard with primary information gathered either by recruiters through conversations with potential candidates (while ensuring you are legally compliant) and also interviews with former employees of the target company (once again ensuring you are legally compliant). These interviews and primary data points are vital to ensure credibility of the battlecards and ensure they are kept as a living document. These are not a 'project', a one-off that you create for a snapshot in time, these are a 'programme' of work that is ongoing. Each battlecard will need to be refreshed periodically. This is important to remember when starting this process, as any old or dead data will reflect poorly on your talent intelligence offerings, so you will need to build ongoing capacity within the team or extended team to ensure this is kept up to date.

It would be remiss to write a section on battlecards without highlighting two individuals who have spearheaded this charge of using battlecards within talent intelligence. Charlotte Christiaanse and Annie Chae with your work on battlecards across Microsoft, Amazon and Philips – you have both set the benchmark and raised the bar of what a commercially-minded talent intelligence function can be.

Always on Intelligence (AoI)

Always on Intelligence (AoI) is a programmatic approach to talent intelligence where you run permanent campaigns of work (always on) against specific competitor groups. This was a programme and a pillar that was most notably launched and driven forward by the brilliant Marlieke Pols and her work while at Philips. Ideally this should align with the marketing intelligence function (if you have one) to be able to give consistent and regular intelligence packs to your senior leadership. Within AoI, it is important to remember from the build phase that this needs to be scalable intelligence by design. So having a wonderful analysis that shows something profound is fantastic but, if it is hugely labour intensive and cannot be scaled to be run across dozens or hundreds of competitors, then it may not be appropriate. Equally, if it is scalable but the analysis takes so long that it cannot be completed in a regular cadence alongside the broader intelligence offering, then it may not be appropriate.

What does this leave then? The type of data you may wan
specific competitor could be (but not limited to):

- job postings and associated analysis both at the macro for trenc
micro for pivot points and changes – it is the anomalies you are in
in, not the business as usual
- sentiment analysis of review sites
- news analysis
- executive movements
- intellectual property review (although this hopefully will already be
caught by an IP team or marketing intelligence)

AoI is a tool that can be built out to act as a talent radar for early-warning
threat detection. If a competitor is opening up a new factory in a location
that is a threat, you can see it coming. If they are looking to pivot as an
organization and threaten your position in a market and show this by hiring
new skills, or if they are looking at expanding into new markets and have
brought in new leaders to disrupt this and threaten your position, you have
it on your radar. If a competitor is looking to ramp up its technical team and
you are exposed as a potential source of hire, you can make your leadership
team aware ahead of time.

If done correctly, AoI can be one of the most powerful weapons in the
talent intelligence arsenal. Not only are you able to see competitor movements, both from a talent and a corporate perspective, ahead of time and
before they have announced to the market, but you also have a direct line of
sight from this research into broader marketing intelligence and have all of
this on display to leadership on a regular basis. This is a fantastic shop
window for the capabilities of your Talent Intelligence offering.

Competitive intelligence

The following section on competitive intelligence is a deep dive from the
brilliant mind of Jay Tarimala. Jay is a talent acquisition professional with
15 plus years of experience in Canada and India. Apart from sourcing, he
has varied experience in recruiting, HR operations, research, proposal
writing, mergers and acquisitions. He is the author of three books: *Sourcing
and Recruitment Handbook*, *Diversity & Inclusion – Getting it Right*, and
Research Methods and Bid Management.

Competitive intelligence (CI) can be useful to map current and emerging competitors' organization structures, compensation and benefit trends, competitor team structures, career growth parameters, etc.

Sources of information gathering

Competitive intelligence can take shape many ways and there are two sources of information gathering.

PRIMARY SOURCES
These can include:

- external buyers
- suppliers
- partners
- research agencies
- competitor staff at trade shows, events
- internal company sales, engineering and R&D teams

SECONDARY SOURCES
These can include:

- social media
- competitor websites
- news releases
- patent and trademark sites
- employer rating sites, etc.

How to go about doing a CI exercise?

A competitor website is the number one source of competitor research. Competitor websites are a veritable treasure of information to understand their operations, priorities, growth avenues, growth levers, partnerships, expansion strategies and product or service portfolio changes. You may also track their press releases, event attendance and event sponsorships to get a better understanding of how they are promoting their brand. If it's a public listed organization, review the 'investor relations' section of their website. You will find their quarterly and annual financial statements, analyst briefings along with corporate governance and social responsibility statements in some cases. Their quarterly and annual reports provide a lot of information about the risks, revenue, margins, compensation and benefits of the top-level management, financial health, subsidiaries, partnerships, growth areas, etc.

Scraping their career section job postings can provide an advanced view of the current and future projects, technology investment areas, skills they are looking to hire for and new location manufacturing/service delivery centre intelligence among others.

The start-up scene gives a view of the emerging competitors that could disrupt your business models and may rewrite the rules of the game. The following are some of the available tools that you could deploy to develop competitive intelligence reports on start-ups or more mature competitors:

- Owler – they provide company data (competitors, revenue, employee numbers, acquisitions and mergers, funding, etc.).

- Pitchbook – you can obtain information related to employee count, office locations, contact information, financing history, financials, top executive names and board members.

- Crunchbase – a platform for finding business information about private and public companies. Crunchbase information includes investments and funding information, founding members and individuals in leadership positions, mergers and acquisitions, news and industry trends.

ALERTS

Google Alerts is an excellent avenue to monitor what your competitors are doing. You just have to type in a company name or any topic of interest and enter the email address of where the alert should be sent to. There are several options like language, frequency and type of alerts (blog, news, etc.).

An alternative to Google Alerts is Talkwalker. It allows you to set up alerts with filters for news, blogs, Twitter, discussion forums only, tracking in 22 different languages, and you can narrow it down to source country as well. The familiar Boolean operators, as discussed earlier, work for this, including wildcard.

You can compare two different companies here and see the top themes, and you can also see the influencers for a specific search query you may have.

MARKETING MESSAGING

Every company will be promoting their product or service for prospects. They will feature testimonials, case studies, YouTube channel and Instagram videos as part of their marketing messages. By tracking such information, you will get to know of their key clients, how they are winning them and their method of building their brand strength.

You may also track their press releases, event attendance (the events they are skipping is also a good data point to track) and event sponsorships to get a better understanding of how they are promoting their brand. Pay attention to what content of theirs gets the most engagement on social media.

TRACKING KEY EMPLOYEES

Review the profiles of your competitor's key employees on LinkedIn and other media in terms of their background, i.e. qualifications, skills, certifications, previous jobs, current role, and responsibilities, etc. Closely track key sales personnel hiring and off-boarding. It could be a sign of booming time ahead, a retention problem or sales not going in the right direction. Also, review sourcing and recruiting team additions or leaving across geographies.

EXECUTIVE MOVES AND UPDATES

Consider the following:

- A gem hidden in plain sight is *New York Times* or *Bloomberg*.
- You can track executive moves by using a very simple string as follows:
  - o site:nytimes.com (CEO OR CFO) (joining OR hired OR stepping OR replaced OR leaving OR resign) "walmart"
  - o site:bloomberg.com (CEO OR CFO) (joining OR hired OR stepping OR replaced OR leaving OR resign) "walmart"
- An addition or a removal of an executive can signal quite a bit. It is important to discuss what this entails and share the learning with the impacted teams.
- For example, if the VP for Product is removed, this could mean there may have been challenges with the speed of product innovation, the features being implemented have not caught the imagination of customers or there may be reliability issues at play. This insight could be a good input for the sales team's competitive positioning or the marketing team's competitive campaigns.

ORGANIZATION CHARTS

Organization charts are pure gold from a competitive research perspective. They depict a reporting or relationship hierarchy and structure and give a good understanding of how decisions are made and the internal dynamics.

From a recruiting perspective, it is quite labour intensive to develop all the organization charts of your competitors, but it could be worth it in the end. Look at:

- theOrg.com
    - https://theorg.com is a neat little organization mapping website and very simple to use. C-suite names, EVPs are listed along with the Board of Director names. When clicking the CEO name, you get a list of direct reports.

CI tools

Following are some of the tools that can be used to review competitor or client websites:

- SimilarWeb
    - If you are looking to review website statistics in terms of the traffic sources, traffic by countries, keywords used, pages per visit, average visit duration, which social media is driving traffic, you can utilize SimilarWeb for this purpose.
    - You can compare one competitor against you or one other competitor as well. The 'free' version gives a good source of information.
- Mediatoolkit
    - This tool can monitor online mentions of your brand in real-time, and will let you know about every article, hashtag or comment mentioning your business. You also can compare with competitors, track current industry topics, find social media influencers, identify engaging posts and analyse brand sentiment.
- VisualPing
    - This tool can monitor a webpage when it changes through an email alert. You can drag the cursor to the section of the page or in full to see if any changes have come about.

- Craft
  - o Craft is an interesting tool to track the past, present and future of companies.
- Builtwith
  - o Builtwith is an excellent tool to find the technology changes on a competitor website in terms of the framework used, widgets, CMS used, email and web hosting providers, advertising networks and languages supported.
  - o Builtwith scans websites and also provides lead generation, competitive analysis and business intelligence tools providing technology adoption, e-commerce data and usage analytics for the internet.
  - o If you are a B2B software provider and you wanted to target competitor's customers, you would first need a list of the clients. Builtwith can provide the list upon demand for a price.
- Twitter
  - o Twitter is a great channel to track your competitor's key personnel or general company progress and update.
- LinkedIn

USING LINKEDIN

Given the wealth of information on LinkedIn, I thought it may be valuable to do a deeper dive to see what we can do from this platform alone. Imagine you have been asked look at a snapshot in time of Company X. Let us call it Quotidian Research.

Quotidian Research has been targeted by your firm as a potential M&A target. Your leadership have tasked you to look at their board, their leadership team and their organizational design and see what you can find from open source information.

I would always recommend, to make your life as easy as possible, to start by going for the low-hanging fruit first. What is the easily available data that you can get fast and consistently to give you some foundation to the work? As Jay so rightly mentioned earlier in this chapter, the corporate website is a great initial starting point. From Quotidian Research's page, we can see: their senior leaders, their board and, rather helpfully, they have published their diversity across the organization.

Public profiles

This gives us some initial macro data for the deeper dive, but it would be important to understand the context of these. We can then look to cross-reference these individuals with other sites such as Viadeo, Xing, etc. to see if these can be enriched further. So, let's dive into LinkedIn. From the leadership's public profiles, you can potentially see:

- their specific tenure at the organization
- any hiring trends from previous firms (all leadership coming from the same previous organization)
- leadership's average tenure across their roles
- if they are alumni from the same schools
- the news and articles they are sharing:
  o expansion news
  o redundancies
  o investment news
  o awards won

Job search

We can use the job search to look at job descriptions/job adverts for any information around reporting structures, areas that are being invested into and growing, areas in times of transformation and salary levelling. Generally, within this type of activity it is *not* the business-as-usual activity that you are looking for. It is the outliers – the data points that are not the norm.

From this we can clearly see some functional organizational structures, some areas of growth, what core verticals Quotidian Research are looking to organize into within healthcare and further investment into the new cloud acquisition sales team due to top-of-the-funnel issues in their managed customer base.

Keeping on the free LinkedIn information, on the job search functionality we can see: total hiring volume, Quotidian Research's top hiring titles, top hiring locations, top hiring functions, their hiring frequency and whether the job was posted in the past 24 hours, past week, month or any time.

Company page

You can then once again use LinkedIn, but this time on the company page. Here we see some excellent features that many are unaware of. As a premium user you can see the following insights:

- total organization headcount and growth rate over 6 or 12 months to one year
- median tenure
- growth, decline and employee distribution by headcount by hiring
- growth, decline and employee distribution by headcount by function

We can also use the jobs side of the portal to really dig into the roles they are hiring for in order to understand any potential pivots as an organization. The jobs that companies are hiring for is a chance to gauge how different businesses might work in new ways in the future as leading (rather than the usual lagging) indicators.

The vast majority of the above was all from the free sections of LinkedIn, with only the premium insights element of the company page being a by-product of a premium paid-for service such as LinkedIn Recruiter. Whether using LinkedIn or any other tool, get comfortable exploring tools and platforms. There are often features and data points within that the average user has not been using on a day-to-day basis.

Summary

So, there you have it – a tour of the types of work you can bring to the table from your talent intelligence function. Now it is important not to be constrained by the above. This is a starting point, not an end point. Use the above as a skeleton of offerings to expand up. Use the location intelligence, the skills analysis, the battlecards and pull them together into a targeted marketing intelligence offering. Tie AoI and the battlecards in with your sales team and create hyper-aggressive competitor battlecards and disruptive hiring plans. We are only limited by our imagination at this point. Remember that people are our biggest asset, but they are also our competitor's biggest asset; lack of access to people is our biggest threat across all markets, business lines and functions. Explore these areas with an open mind and you will find new and exciting product offerings for your teams.

TOBY'S TAKEAWAYS

- Structuring your project intake and project delivery can bring a great deal of control, clarity and the ability to scale, but it is not a given in all teams.

- Regardless of team set-up and location, be clear about who is your key customer, as that will allow you to create a service offering appropriate for their needs.

- The breadth of project offerings is very large. At this stage we are only limited by our own imaginations.

- There is a vast amount of publicly available data out there. Get comfortable with searching for, aggregating, digesting and providing critical review of this as early in your development as possible.

EXAMPLE PROJECT PLAN

Note: data is fictitious for this example.

What is the key issue we are trying to resolve?

We are looking to expand our headcount by 900 in the next 12 months and 5000 in the next five years. We do not know if the current location is feasible for this growth, the potential financial impact or the competitor landscape we face. There are five potential growth locations identified close to customers.

This is estimated to be a $500 million investment in headcount growth and a further $1.2 billion in new infrastructure and facilities to enable the $5 billion business growth we have forecast.

This research will both de-risk that decision and ensure the growth of the organization.

What are the key data points needed to effect the decision point?

1 Ease of access to talent now and in the future

2 Total weighted cost

3 Labour market stability

4 Competitor growth in location

Who are the key stakeholders that need to be informed through this process?

Business leader, HRBP, Real Estate, Finance

Who are the key support teams that need to be engaged for data through this process?

Finance, real estate, finance/tax, HR analytics, talent acquisition

What is the confidentiality level of the project?

Highly Confidential, Restricted to Project team.

What is the measurable impact of this research and what are the metrics for success?

With the costs estimated to be a $500 million investment in headcount growth and a $1.2 billion in new infrastructure and facilities, we estimate a $200 million variance between locations on the bottom line of the business and an estimated $150 million impact of improved empty seat time and reduced attrition

What parameters are in/out of scope?

In scope: Talent/skill supply, talent demand, salary cost, total headcount cost, competitor organizational growth and changes in hiring, competitor salary analysis, market attrition rate, funnel metric conversion rates, diversity make up of market and specific roles, real estate cost, infrastructure stability, tax incentives in given location. Across five designated potential locations while reviewing remote working opportunities
Out of scope: Data points outside of the United States

What is the timescale needed for delivery?

Decision review meeting in two months; bi-weekly update calls to be arranged throughout.

Endnotes

1 US Army (2006) 'Human Intelligence Collector Operations', September, fas.org/irp/doddir/army/fm2-22-3.pdf (archived at https://perma.cc/3Z8T-H6VT)

2 UK College of Policing (2022) 'UK College of Policing Intelligence Report', first published 24 August 2015, updated 26 January 2022, www.college.police.uk/app/intelligence-management/intelligence-report (archived at https://perma.cc/QF43-K49M)

06

Metrics for success and KPIs

A big thank you to Kim Bryan and Teresa Wykes for your help and support across this chapter. Your insights were invaluable.

We now have an appreciation of what the problem statements and red flags can be, along with some of the types of product and service offerings that can be created to address these needs. But, as with any business function, the old adage of 'what gets measured gets done' rings true. With that in mind, it is vitally important to set yourself up for success by measuring parameters that drive your capability forward while demonstrating an impact that your business is aligned with. Now, before we dive into the metrics and key performance indicators (KPIs) themselves, it is important to ask what metrics and KPIs are, why we have them and how we capture and measure them. Within this chapter we will primarily focus on metrics and KPIs associated with core Talent Intelligence teams and sourcing intelligence activities.

What are metrics and KPIs?

Broadly speaking, both metrics and KPIs are there to achieve a similar end goal: to track and measure your organization's health and progress. That is where the similarity ends.

Metrics are the business-as-usual measures of productivity and process flows. They will be the type of efficiency targets that will often have industry benchmarks. They are often static and organized by an activity or process.

KPIs are laser focused. They are specific against strategic targets. They are there to measure your progress against the most important team goals and objectives. KPIs will be set and reset over time and will often follow the SMART methodology of being Specific, Measurable, Achievable, Realistic and Timebound.

Why do we need metrics?

Now on the face of it, this sounds like a somewhat silly question as it is likely that every role you have ever had, every team you have been in, every function and every organization has had clear metrics and KPIs. Fundamentally knowing and measuring the right metrics will help you achieve results faster, build business and customer trust, develop your offering and use them to differentiate your approach/services from what the rest of talent acquisition or other data talent or data teams provide.

Building effective metrics and monitoring these will allow you to see any trends across your capability, foresee risks ahead in the road, while looking at the productivity, speed and quality of the work you are producing. This structure allows you to build a crisp management information dashboard to be able to report up and out in a repeatable and consistent manner. This data set and reporting not only helps to build trust with stakeholders but also can be used operationally with your team to see team health and capacity crunches in the future and to discuss any anomalies. This transparency on metrics will allow your team to all pull in the same direction. They will know why these metrics are important and how their work aligns and impacts the metrics.

As we will discuss in more detail later in the chapter, you may wish to track and measure certain metrics (such as measurable business impact value, number of projects completed or average project duration) but you may not want that as a KPI with targets and goals attached as that may drive the wrong behaviours.

How do we capture the data?

This element of a Talent Intelligence function's development is often missed or undervalued. When you are an individual setting up a talent intelligence capability it is relatively easy to keep track of your workload and your deliverables. You have things stored in your usual places; you know what projects are at what stages; you know what you have to deliver and have everything on track. This though has two main pitfalls: it is not scalable and it is very unlikely to be auditable and trackable from which to be able to drive consistent KPIs and metrics. With this in mind, it is vital to try to build a system and process for project delivery and data point capture that is scalable and auditable as early as possible.

Now what that platform or process is can vary wildly. Generally, I have been a fan of reusing and repurposing existing platforms that are already in the organization, as this has meant I can move faster within platforms and environments that have already been through information security checks, procurement, onboarding and so on, so there is very little barrier to entry. It is perfectly possible to run talent intelligence workflows through existing candidate relationship management (CRM) systems or through project management platforms. The workflow discussed in Chapter 5 is relatively simple and can be configured in most systems. What you are looking for in a system is one that tracks the elements through the process and allows you to export the data or has built-in analysis or dashboarding.

The type of values/fields I would normally look to track and monitor would be fairly explicit as this allows for greater tracking and data insights. This can absolutely feel like it is overkill if you are a small team or a newly established team where everyone has visibility on each other's work. But having this granularity and structure puts the infrastructure in from the start to enable you to scale without having to redesign your systems, processes and tooling as you build.

These values and fields would broadly fall into three buckets: project values and fields; business values and fields; and operational values and fields.

Project values and fields

For the project values and fields, I may consider the following:

- Project name
  - What is the title of the project? This should be in a consistent format across all projects to allow customer consistency and also ease of search and retrieval
- Project description
  - I would usually recommend having two project description fields: one that holds the full description and is explicit, which is for use for the project team to have a view of the detail within a project without

diving into the full project plan; the second I refer to as the 'project synopsis', i.e a short and brief summary of the project. This should be more general and give less detail than the earlier project description. This synopsis can be used in comms to stakeholders to give an overview of project pipeline or workload

- Project owner
  - o Who is the owner of the project and its delivery?
- Project status
  - o This could be: intake/in process/project delivered/post-project NPS completed/on hold/cancelled/rejected due to scope/rejected due to capacity
- Project start date
- Project estimated delivery date
- Project delivery date
  - o The reason to have both estimated delivery date and delivery date is to be able to track your project over-run. Are you able to accurately predict how long work should take and account for buffer capacity? This is vital to build trust with the customer and also to build out future team capacity and workload management
- Priority
  - o As per the prioritization matrix discussed in Chapter 5
- Type of project
  - o It is important to capture the type of project you are doing to see where your time is spent. This could be location studies, desktop research, organizational benchmarking, M&A intelligence, cultural assessment, competitor analysis, etc.
- Confidentiality level
  - o What is the confidentiality level of this work? Highly confidential, restricted to project team, restricted to talent intelligence, restricted to leadership, open access, etc.
- Level of importance
  - o As per the prioritization matrix discussed in Chapter 5
- Urgency
  - o As per the prioritization matrix discussed in Chapter 5

- Partner teams
  - o What teams are you partnering with? Who are the stakeholders for the project?

Business values and fields

For the business values and fields, I may consider the following:

- Organization
  - o What business line/organization does the work align to?
- Sponsor and customer level
  - o What grade/level is the sponsor and customer of this project? This is vital to ensure you are working on projects that tie in at the appropriate level within the organization
- Sponsor and customer name/alias
- Business impact value
  - o The business articulated impact value or investment value of the project you are working on
- Core strategic goal
  - o Articulate and capture how projects align to your/your organization's core strategic goals. If projects are not aligning, really question why you are working on them
- Headcount impacted
  - o This gives a good understanding of the scale of the project you are working on
- Average salary of headcount impacted
  - o To be used in conjunction with the total headcount impacted to give a 'headcount investment' figure for new sites, expansion planning, etc. This is simply the total headcount impacted multiplied by the average salary of those impacted. This once again aids in seeing scale of work impacted
- Number of locations in scope
  - o This gives a sense of scale and complexity to the problem you are facing. This can also be used as a data point for external benchmarking of your services versus research firms or consulting firms for cost avoidance goals

- Number of different job categories in scope
  - o This gives a sense of scale and complexity to the problem you are facing

Operational Values and fields

For the operational values and fields, I may consider the following:

- Headcount
  - o The headcount needed to complete a project. I have always allowed this to be a fractional value to reflect time spent on a project e.g. 1.5 meaning one person full time and one person for 50 per cent of the project. This is important to capture if you are looking to create research firm/consultancy avoidance benchmarking data
- Project pillar
  - o How is your work aligning within your team? Is it falling into consulting, analytics, sourcing intelligence, candidate listening? Even if you are starting a team from scratch, and are alone, I would recommend creating project pillars to see where you are spending your time

Once you have your parameters set in your chosen system, it is important to make any kind of reporting or dashboard analysis process as seamless and automated as possible. This both improves the quality of the management information, as there will be less human intervention and error, and improves the speed of service as everything should be kept as real time as possible. It also means you are more likely to review more frequently as there is less heavy lifting involved with pulling together any management information.

What are the metrics for success?

This is currently one of the most hotly debated areas within Talent Intelligence. The reason for this is twofold: first, because this is still such a new space, so standardized benchmarks and success metrics are not in place across the industry; and, secondly, because many talent intelligence capabilities and Talent Intelligence functions are being stood up in other functions, such as talent acquisition, and then they try to give line of sight to the larger teams' goals and KPIs. This brings an innate friction given the different mechanisms and operating rhythms of the two worlds.

For the sake of clarity, I will break metrics for success and KPIs into two main bucketed groups: those for sourcing intelligence and those for talent intelligence consulting. Within this context I will use the SI and TI definitions and explanations as we discussed in Chapter 3. It is worth noting many Talent Intelligence teams are conducting a large amount of sourcing intelligence activities so you may well want to adopt some of these metrics if appropriate.

The most important thing to remember across all of this is to ensure you are tracking elements that drive impact – not simply elements that drive activity. For example, a very simple straightforward measure that many teams will start with is 'number of projects completed'. Now in of itself this should not be a bad metric, especially if you are tying the work to having the right level of customer, the defined measurable business impact, aligned to strategic goals, etc. However, with this KPI what you are really saying to a team member is that I value activity over impact: two projects completed is better than one, four is better than two and so on. This will drive team members to:

- complete projects as fast as possible rather than as impactfully and holistically as possible
- look for low-hanging fruit vanity projects that they can pass through on paper as appropriate (by say aligning it to a strategic goal) but they know is not truly a strategic project or impacting for the greater good
- look to run too many projects simultaneously to increase the overall delivery number (and likely either burn out or deliver sub-standard work)

The one adage to remember throughout this is that KPIs will drive the team's behaviours. Whatever you set will drive the energies, efforts and results from the team. This has the potential to be hugely beneficial but also will have side effects if not considered thoroughly.

Sourcing intelligence (SI)

By design, sourcing intelligence naturally sits very close to sourcing and recruitment. In fact, you will often see SI being seen as a mechanism to be a force multiplier for a sourcing or recruiting function. Due to this you will often see a lot of sourcing intelligence teams have success metrics and KPIs directly aligned to sourcing and recruiting goals.

Some common metrics include:

- total number of requisitions impacted
- total number of candidates generated
- total number of placements made
- total number of research papers delivered

Now these can be fantastic KPIs. They give a clear line of sight to your work and potential impact and give a clear route for team and headcount increase.

However, the main difficulty across all most of these KPIs (total number of requisitions/candidates/placements) is definitions and systems. Often, we get caught up in the nuances and stuck in the weeds. What do you mean by 'impacted'? What does a generated candidate mean: one new to the system or one new to the requisition? What if it was a candidate resurfaced/resurrected? What if they were inactive on a requisition and had been missed?

You will also run the risk of coming into active conflict with your customer base as your respective KPIs may be misaligned; for example, if a sourcing team is tasked with unearthing and generating candidates and then you support them with work. Will they want to highlight that you found the candidates? Or will they look to drive their own candidate pipeline to achieve their own KPIs? Remember that KPIs drive behaviours.

Then you layer on top of that the already difficult task of tracking placements made, and candidates sourced, that is already a struggle for most sourcing teams to do in a clean manner with duplication of candidate profiles, duplicative systems, duplicative requisitions and candidates being run off platform. If you are being tasked with goals such as the above, be prepared to dedicate a large amount of capacity to track, monitor and audit all engagements and associated placements.

ALTERNATIVE SUCCESS METRICS AND KPIS

Alternatives to think about could be:

- average Net Promoter Score (NPS) or Customer Satisfaction Score
- cost avoidance versus research firms
- time savings to customer (and associated cost saving)
- repeat business
- recruitment marketing spend cost reduction
- cost savings on agency fees

- reduced time to hire/reduced empty seat time
- closure of historical requisitions

With all KPIs and metrics, think about what you want to drive as a behaviour and keep the holy trinity of time, quality and cost in terms of what you are measuring. How are you saving time? How are you improving or measuring quality? How are you reducing cost or increasing value?

Talent intelligence consulting (TIC)

For TIC I would say you have operating KPIs, literally the key indicators to see how you are performing as a function. Then you have the actual team goals. For me, they can and should be aligned, but not everything you track needs to be a KPI. If you have transactional KPIs you will have transactional behaviours.

For me, the operating metrics should be used to see how the team is functioning. Are the mechanisms in place working? What are the recurrent issues or bottlenecks? They are not used to drive behavioural change or aligned to any goals in the same way that your KPIs should.

Metrics

The type of metrics I would usually measure and have management information dashboards created against would be things such as:

- project overrun (do you deliver projects when you say you will?)
- time to completion
- count of: total number of projects, number of projects aligned to strategic goals/specific business units/functions, number of projects rejected due to capacity, number of projects by customer level or number of projects by project sponsor level
- from the post-project feedback session
  - o communication of team
  - o timeliness of delivery
  - o accuracy of the research

ALTERNATIVE SUCCESS METRICS AND KPIS TO THINK ABOUT COULD BE:
These could include:

- number of repeat requests/repeat business of senior stakeholders
- business articulated financial/commercial impact
- cost avoidance (versus research firms/external partners and consulting rates)
- customer expansion (number of projects in new customer groups)
- levelling (number of projects at a target level within the organization)
- headcount investment from research conducted

As discussed previously, you should look to build dashboard tracking and reporting mechanisms that are as automated and real time as possible. This means you can communicate out your metrics, successes and KPI reporting at any time for any need.

Communication mechanism

Once you have the systems or processes in place to track and capture the KPIs and success metrics that are important to your growth and goals, your function's goals and your organizations goals, it is important to think about how you will report this back out to customers/stakeholders. This normally will have two main elements: an overall communications strategy and then a more targeted business review process. In this section we will look into both of these in more detail.

Communications

Having a communications strategy would sound strange at first in a talent intelligence team but I think it is arguably the single biggest missed opportunity for most teams. If your talent intelligence team's mission is to enable and empower your customer teams with the right market data, analysis and intelligence, at the right time to drive impactful strategic decisions, then your communication strategy will enable the team to achieve their mission and goals by providing effective communication for stakeholders as well as internal collaboration and organization.

The communication strategy can be broken into two categories: internal communication, which focuses on communication within the TI team; and external communication which focuses on any of your teams' stakeholders outside the team with a sub-section of marketing awareness.

INTERNAL

Your internal communications strategy should be targeted to the talent intelligence team and focused on the rhythm of business and reporting, to ensure team flow is in order. This means making sure all meeting cadence and agendas are up to date, as well as reviewing reporting mechanisms in comparison to the organization and realigning if needed. Within this internal communication would be ownership of all business reviews, but also importantly tying into other partner organizations' business reviews to ensure the talent intelligence team, and your work, is represented across your stakeholder and partner base.

EXTERNAL

The external communication strategy should target your customers and partners. The external communication strategy should include the following:

- Reporting and communicating to senior leaders on an efficient and consistent basis. This consists of identifying the correct stakeholders to be receiving your communications, as well as creating targeted communications to be sent. In addition, labour market trends should be sent out on a regular basis, either monthly or bi-monthly. You should put tracking methods into place and use them to make sure all content is being received properly; adjustments should be made based on tracking results. The external communication strategy should also include an awareness campaign. This campaign can be used to raise awareness to senior leaders about the work and capabilities that your function do and have, with an end goal of more projects requested and customer expansion.

- The external communications can include a newsletter(s). The newsletter can be sent out on monthly basis providing stakeholders with updates about the team, any useful information, any training or events to attend, and much more. This should be sent to a targeted list of stakeholders that will be monitored and updated if needed.

Business reviews

Business reviews are the most common mechanism to communicate any update on the function's health to your stakeholder group. Whether you choose to run these as weekly business reviews (WBRs), monthly business reviews (MBRs), quarterly business reviews (QBRs) or yearly business reviews (YBRs) will depend on the rhythm of your business, but I would strongly suggest that if your business rhythm is QBR and YBR only that you look at an additional communications mechanism within each quarterly period.

WHAT IS A BR AND WHAT SHOULD BE INCLUDED?

A BR is a meeting (or at minimum a standardized email, but I would recommend meeting) where you and a partner meet with your customer to discuss their business and review how the preceding period has gone, as well as looking to the future to see what can be improved, what is on your roadmap and how you can add more value in the next given period (be it week, month, quarter or year depending on the review cycle).

The sort of agenda items to look to include could be:

- executive summary
- goals update
- project highlights
- lowlights/learnings
- strategic obstacles and challenges
- roadmap/path forward

The benefits of this review cycle are many; one of the primary benefits though is the chance to review, alignment and realignment on priorities and goals. Businesses move fast and the goals can often be somewhat fluid. This is a chance to ensure everyone is still singing from the same song sheet and aligned in pulling in the same direction. Similarly, this is a fantastic opportunity to give a strategic view of your partnership with the customer (internal or external). It is so easy to become entangled by the day-to-day activities and lose sight of the strategic partnership. This BR gives a chance to review and ensure you are all working at the correct level. Tied into this, the BR is an excellent opportunity to reinforce and build trust.

Both the regular face time and regular communication cadence and the transparency of the BR process mean that they are a fantastic mechanism for building relationships and trust with your core customer base. BRs are also great for capturing customer feedback on how things are going. It gives them a chance to raise any topics and personalize the relationship and ensures the voice of the customer is heard and at the core of your offering.

If you are running with a quarterly business review cycle I would also recommend both more regular informal check-ins, to confirm prioritization of work and workload alignment, but also creating a regular communication each month to update stakeholders on projects delivered and any other relevant news. This increases your touch points with the customer base and both informs them but also invites communication back in between QBR sessions. This monthly communication plan can rapidly develop into a whole communications roadmap and comms/knowledge management strategy.

Summary

Within this chapter we have touched on a few versions of success metrics and KPIs. At their heart though they should be very personal to you, your team, your function and your organization.

You need to ensure you build the metrics that track and monitor what the customers care about and goals and KPIs that will challenge you and drive the behaviours you want to see across the team. Remember that once goals are signed off and KPIs aligned, this also gives you direction and permission to prioritize ruthlessly to align your work to these goals. Ensure they are pulling you in the direction of travel in which you want to take the Talent Intelligence function.

From a communications perspective, make sure you are being proactive and telling the business and the leaders of your successes. Give the business the information they need to allow them to be your cheerleaders and evangelists. Be clear and transparent about the challenges and open about the failings and lessons learnt. Your communications strategy and its deployment can be an opportunity to reinforce relationships, earn trust and business develop into new areas. As discussed earlier in the book, do this with a clear talent intelligence brand and brand positioning.

TOBY'S TAKEAWAYS

- Be clear about what you want to achieve with your metrics, goals and KPIs. What you set will drive the direction and activity of the team.

- Success can mean very different things for different teams. There is no right or wrong; it is all contextual to you and your organization.

- Success is often not seen by the leadership or stakeholders: be deliberate about how you communicate out to your stakeholders and build this capacity into the team.

07

Where to sit the TI function within organizations

In Chapter 17 we will discuss more about potential future states of the function, industry and alternative reporting structures in more detail. Within this chapter we will look at the current state and the various options and models that people are adopting.

Where to sit the Talent Intelligence function has been one of the hottest and most common discussions across the field in the last few years. In the 2021 Talent Intelligence Collective Benchmarking Survey, over 50 per cent of existing Talent Intelligence functions said they reported into a Talent Acquisition function, but only 22 per cent said that they thought this is where they should report into. The most interesting element, however, is when you look at the spread of where respondents thought that they should report into: Talent Acquisition, Centralized Intelligence, Strategy and HR/People Strategy all received between 18 to 22 per cent of the votes, with the remainder being in HR Analytics or Executive Recruitment.[1]

I would argue that the primary reason for the debate is the huge variance in Talent Intelligence functional design, with teams having very different skills, remits and desired future states. This is all to be expected within an industry at its infancy. Nevertheless, understanding the potential context of sitting within functions is important.

Let us first look at the most common scenario, having Talent Intelligence based in Talent Acquisition.

Talent Intelligence based in Talent Acquisition

As discussed previously, this is a natural starting point for a lot of functions as they look to initially influence the sourcing and recruiting activities using

Sourcing Intelligence. There is a natural affinity from a product knowledge and subject matter expertise with a large amount of crossover. As we will discuss in Chapters 11 and 12, the skills needed within Talent Intelligence can often resonate with those in Talent Acquisition and the two functions can absolutely offer career pathing opportunities within each other.

If sitting within Talent Acquisition, as well as the KPIs and goals as previously discussed in Chapter 6, it is very important to be really clear about how you align the 'go to market' mechanism for Talent Intelligence. This is the mechanism you use to reach your customer base (as previously discussed) and ensure both a clear demand signal for incoming work but also ensure a clear route to customer for completed projects and feedback. The reason that this is so important is that often Talent Acquisition is focused on the short- and medium-term delivery of current and near-future recruitment needs. This is vital activity but can leave you exposed if this is your only demand signal for strategic Talent Intelligence work, as the conversations that are being engaged with may only extend a quarter or two into the future. This can be hugely useful for Sourcing Intelligence but can leave little time for Talent Intelligence to be able to align, complete work and deliver in time for any meaningful impact.

To be clear, this is not to say that there are not Talent Acquisition teams out there looking at future state workforce planning in a strategic manner, of course there are, and in those teams an alignment for Talent Intelligence could and would be hugely beneficial. It is also vital to make sure Talent Acquisition are working in tight alignment, whether nested functionally or TA being serviced as a customer and partner organization. There are recruiters capturing primary intelligence on every call, every single day, that can flow back up and be scaled and aggregated by Talent Intelligence. The voice of talent acquisition (VoTA) is absolutely vital to incorporate into as much work as possible to give a true view of what is happening on the ground.

Whether it is looking at future location feasibility, growth planning, DEI sourcing feasibility or the future talent gap to name but a few, Talent Acquisition will be integral to very many elements within a Talent Intelligence team's output, offerings and customer alignment and sitting your function within TA can keep you close to the market customer.

Talent Intelligence based in HR Analytics

HR Analytics is a powerful home for any Talent Intelligence function. Over the last few years, HR analytics teams have rapidly been evolving their offerings to also have visibility to the external labour market. Using talent intelligence allows HR analytics functions to set the context for their outputs, whether that is benchmarking internal metrics and reporting, looking at the feasibility of goals, or setting the feasibility of HR strategies.

There are a number of benefits of sitting within HR Analytics. As mentioned earlier, understanding the context of existing reporting or goals setting is hugely valuable to any HR organization. This holistic view will enable faster, more accurate and more feasible goal setting. It will enable the HR leadership to have a stronger and more credible conversation with leadership, especially in this highly volatile and uncertain labour market.

In most organizations, HR Analytics already has a very clear route to customers. They are levelled at a senior, strategic and impactful layer within the organization, giving any Talent Intelligence function an instant route into key strategic decision-making customers. This is a fantastic by-product of the Talent Intelligence team alignment that can fast track the evolution, investment and impact of the function.

Also, by being within this function, you can better align your technical platforms to look to have a cleaner data management and engineering architecture. Having greater clarity and consistency across your data sets will enable your Talent Intelligence function to have a truly impactful holistic view. You can improve business efficiency, for example, by considering the following:

- Are we able to predict potential attrition issues by far more accurately being to overlay with competitor demand, external candidate sentiment analysis or external salary benchmarking due to market fluctuations?

- Can we look at forecast start data for seasonal work or hourly workers, look at the channel conversion metrics, look at pipeline health and combine with external conditions such as competitor hiring, salary fluctuations or even the weather forecast data to see if we are more or less likely to hit this forecast start level?

- Are our diversity targets both feasible in market or are there opportunities to improve given the external diversity landscape?

- Do we have the appropriate span of control and organization levelling and how does this compare to our competitors?

There can be challenges though. As we will discuss in Chapter 8, the maturity curve of HR Analytics and Talent Intelligence functions are not always aligned, with a possible friction between the two. The skill sets within the two functions (to be discussed in Chapter 11) can be quite different and depending upon the leadership, evolution and vision, this can either been highly complementary or challenging.

Across the board within HR there are problems and challenges that can be enhanced using external labour market information. This is the value that talent intelligence can provide and it can be argued that this can be maximized by placing within HR Analytics.

Talent Intelligence based in Executive Recruitment

We see several Talent Intelligence teams being created within Executive Recruitment functions. This is largely due to two main reasons: first, the levelling of the organization and their customer base; and, secondly, external research has a natural home within Executive Recruitment.

From a customer base perspective, Executive Recruitment ties in at a very senior level within organizations and these leaders often look to their trusted advisers (Executive Recruitment in this case) for advice and answers. This gives an instant route to market and customer base for any talent intelligence capability or Talent Intelligence function that sits within Executive Recruitment.

Within Executive Recruitment, high-level competitive intelligence, market and industry intelligence and organizational design has been the core of their delivery for many years. This means that using this as a product range base and then expanding out to broader Talent Intelligence offerings becomes a relatively easy pivot.

The skills needed within both functions align very closely (as we will discuss in Chapter 11 in more detail), with both needing highly consultative problem-solving skills, but with Talent Intelligence often needing a heavier focus on raw data and data analytics.

There are challenges associated with this placement. The first is the nature of the data. By its nature, Executive Recruitment and the associated research is focused closely on the individual and the micro-level. Whether looking at market mapping, organizational design, M&A strategy and so on, they are looking at individuals and their relationships to each other. This means that they may not have the systems, processes or tooling to look at the macro level data needed for Talent Intelligence. This though is an easy problem to solve. One way of solving this is to have a fully ringfenced Talent Intelligence subteam within ER. This gives you the relationships and route to customer benefit while allowing you to build a specialized TI function with their own systems, processes, tools, skills and team-aligned metrics, goals and KPIs.

Talent Intelligence based in Strategic Workforce Planning

Strategic workforce planning (SWP) is a process of strategically looking at and analysing your current state and future state as an organization, and not only seeing the gap in place but also designing interventions and solutions (usually via Talent Management) for the organization to achieve the desired future state. For clarity, operational workforce planning will often be completed by existing activities and roles within roles in Human Resources and be focused on the short- to medium-term workforce planning. But you will often see SWP as a specialized and dedicated function to look further out to the future.

SWP makes for a natural partner for Talent Intelligence as a customer or as a function to be sat within. By its nature, the SWP process sits in a timeframe, a customer base and a mechanism of strategic importance that ties in closely with TI. You are by default looking at highly strategic planning and decision-making, so partnering this process and enriching it with external labour market intelligence is highly valuable.

Talent Intelligence based in Centralized Intelligence

One of the more popular theories at present is to sit Talent Intelligence within a Centralized Intelligence function, but what does this really mean? Centralized Intelligence is a conceptual function, drawing in expertise from across the organization into a central team. This often aligns with a centralized data strategy of having data brought together into central data lakes, rather than decentralized out in pockets in the business. This centralized data allows for new holistic thinking at a pan-silo nature. Even though centralization of data has certainly caught on, and more companies are embracing it, we still largely see insights and intelligence being decentralized with actionable insights being delivered closer to the business.

Now, although true centralized intelligence is still a pipe dream in most organizations, there are still routes forward being forged at present.

As it stands currently, I am not aware of any Talent Intelligence function sitting within a Centralized Intelligence team but, as we saw in the Talent

Intelligence Collective Benchmarking Survey, around 20 per cent of respondents would like to see this. We will explore this deeper in Chapter 17 around potential future state models but let's dig into this concept a little more on current state.

What would be considered in Centralized Intelligence?

Although Talent Intelligence as a function has not yet found a home in other intelligence functions within organizations, talent intelligence as an activity surely has. Whether within Competitor Intelligence, Market Intelligence, Marketing Intelligence or Business Intelligence, we are seeing numerous instances where teams are building out this labour market intelligence muscle without necessarily knowing about Talent Intelligence as a concept.

First let's clarify what we mean by the above:

- Competitor Intelligence is the result of a company's efforts to gather, analyse and derive intelligence from any information about a competitor's industry, footprint and competitive products and services.

- Market Intelligence is very similar information as above, but this time rather than dissecting by competitor first, you are market-driven and looking at any intelligence relevant to a company's market – customer trends, competitor and customer monitoring, gathered and analysed.

- Marketing Intelligence, often used interchangeably with Market Intelligence, sometimes refers more to primary market research but is generally seen to be more targeted to specific business units, product lines and launches, etc.

- Business Intelligence is a much broader term that often encompasses all technologies, processes, data engineering, data warehousing, data mining and analysis, performance benchmarking and data visualization that enable organizations to make better decisions.

Now we are currently witnessing a talent gap the like of which has not been seen in the market for a hundred years. This means that leaders across their organizations are looking to their various trusted advisers to better understand the context. This could be a Market Intelligence team to better understand talent flows in the market and any talent hotspots or it could be a Competitor Intelligence team to dig into competitors and understand how they are managing to pull their talent out (organizational design, compensation and benefits, remote working policies, rapid growth, etc.). This all feels very much like talent intelligence, doesn't it? If there is not an existing Talent Intelligence function in place, or a talent intelligence capability visible, then many of these teams will look to answer these questions as best they can.

Intelligence cadence

One of the biggest differences between the above and traditional talent intelligence is the cadence of the work. Most other intelligence functions are designed around programmatic work that is ongoing. It is there to provide regular cadence of information in a standardized and structured way. This is in stark contrast to talent intelligence, which is often geared around project-based work and specific deep dives. However, as we discussed in Chapter 5, Always on Intelligence (AoI) is a programmatic approach to talent intelligence where you run permanent campaigns of work (always on) against specific competitor groups. This finds a natural ally with Competitor Intelligence and Market and Marketing Intelligence in particular. Being able to combine the Competitor, Market and Marketing Intelligence with targeted talent intelligence gives a holistic view of both the 'what' is happening but also the 'why' it is happening.

Also, at a goal and directional level, this alignment can often work if you want a more strategically focused Talent Intelligence function. Common goals for marketing or competitive intelligence include:

- growing your existing market share
- strengthening of your corporate brand.
- improving your overall brand awareness.
- determining potential new markets to enter.
- seeing gaps in the market and developing new product lines to match these

Talent Intelligence can both align with these very strongly but also mirror these across the talent landscape. For example:

- Grow your existing comparative talent market share (not total numbers, but consider if you are increasing your share proportionately)
- Strengthening of your employer brand – using candidate listening, sentiment analysis, etc. to confirm your positioning and working with recruitment marketing to ensure employer value proposition alignment

- Improving your overall talent brand awareness – how are you being perceived by your targeted talent populations? Could you run focus groups or primary research to dig into this more?

- Determining potential new talent markets to enter – where are the skills based versus your footprint? What are the opportunities that arise if you look to move to remote first or return to office first?

- Seeing gaps in the market and developing new product lines to match these – what are candidates looking for from jobs? What are they searching for and how does that align? How are competitors hiring – are they pivoting their skill sets, their geographic footprint or their product offering?

Overall, there are a lot of positives from aligning Talent Intelligence within existing intelligence functions. The skills are very similar in data analytics and storytelling with data, all to be discussed more in Chapter 11 (albeit often focused on programme rather than project, but very transferable); there is a clear and structured route to the internal stakeholders; there is a functional maturity that they can often bring.

Summary

No matter what function you are aligned to, it does not necessarily limit your reach or potential impact. Be clear about the customer, their needs, the most appropriate route to them and understand the decision mechanisms in your organization that you would like to inject talent intelligence into. As with the product offering and customer clarification, perform a work back exercise to see what the desired future state is and work backwards to ensure everything is aligned to you and the function reaching that future state. If your organization, function or team are misaligned, you need to stop and assess whether this future state or the alignment are wrong. Or, if all correct, be clear about how you will communicate the misalignment and mitigate any future risks this may pose.

TOBY'S TAKEAWAYS

- You may not have control over where your function is set up. Be clear, though, about the benefits, risks and opportunities of being housed where you are.

- Do not be limited. There is opportunity all around us with functions wanting to partner, support and collaborate.

- Nothing is fixed. Teams evolve; offerings mature; functions align. It is very unlikely that any Talent Intelligence function created today will have the same 'home' in five years' time, let alone in ten years.

- To reiterate: no matter what function you are aligned to, it does not necessarily limit your reach or potential impact. Be bold, be brave and push the boundaries.

Endnote

1 The Talent Intelligence Collective 2021 Benchmarking Survey. See resources from the Talent Intelligence Collective at: www.koganpage.com/talent-intelligence (archived at https://perma.cc/XFZ7-3AAC).

08

Talent intelligence maturity model

In this chapter, we are going to look at a Talent Intelligence maturity model and what to expect as you drive though this model. We will look at how scrappy things can feel at first, how you can look to position and reposition yourself as a trusted adviser as you develop your offering and look at what a mature state Talent Intelligence function or talent intelligence offering could look like. Before we dive into the model fully, I wanted to call out two areas in particular that are worth thinking about: the early days and the roadmap to being a trusted adviser.

Jack-of-all-trades

In the first few days, weeks and months of setting up any talent intelligence capability, it can feel very messy. You are pulled in all directions and you are trying to build the plane as you fly it. You are delivering work while also trying to set your mission, your vision, your goals, your systems, processes, tools, skills gaps, product offering, define your customer base and so on. Everyone is excited to see what this new concept and offering is, so they will be chomping at the bit to work with you.

Demand will be high, but equally they won't have necessarily worked with a Talent Intelligence team before so you will spend a lot of time educating the stakeholders. They will have questions such as:

- What is Talent Intelligence?
- How does it align and how do we measure impact?
- How can it help solve my problems?

Equally, you will need to set expectations about things such as:

- what Talent Intelligence is not
- what is out of scope
- what timeframe is realistic
- what workload is manageable at any one time
- explaining that there is not a hidden source of truth with unknown data sources that will give them all their answers at the drop of a hat

Know that during this period it is perfectly normal to feel like you are failing. You are spread thin and you do not feel like you're overdelivering in any given area; you can see so much opportunity and need but just cannot do it all. You are the definition of a jack-of-all-trades – having to get stuck into anything and everything from a talent intelligence stance. With this, though, know two very important things:

1 Remember the true meaning of 'jack-of-all-trades'. We often associate 'a jack-of-all-trades is a master of none' with negative connotations. It is often used as reference to someone who has dabbled in many skills, rather than gaining expertise by focusing on one. But it is important to remember the full saying 'a jack-of-all-trades is a master of none, but oftentimes better than a master of one'. Do not fear this scrappy period. You will move faster, learn more skills and develop your offering faster than at any other time in your function's development. Things may not be as robust as if you had specialists building that infrastructure, the data engineering, the data visualization and so on, but you will find a path forward and you will set the tone to build these things out more robustly in the future.

2 Do not be alarmed: this storming phase is normal and in fact aligns closely with the forming–storming–norming–performing model of group development. Things will focus as you scale and mature.

Trusted adviser

A 'trusted adviser' is a name given to an individual, a team or a company that is seen as a core strategic partner rather than a support team or a vendor. You will be at the table for all core strategic decisions and be consulted ahead of time rather than seeing the reactive output of those meetings. Arguably, there are no shortcuts to becoming a trusted adviser as at its core is trust which is built up over time and working together. However, there is a structured path you should consider in order to see how close you are to reaching that point.

I would argue that there are four main role developments and evolutions that will set you up for success as a talent intelligence trusted adviser.

An overview of the path is as shown in Figure 8.1.

FIGURE 8.1   The path to trusted adviser status: Provider > Problem Solver > Insight Generator > Trusted Adviser

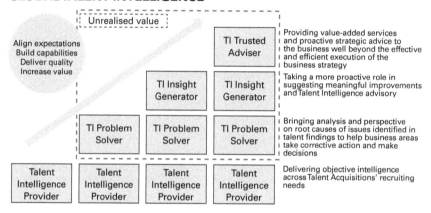

It is in the gap between the Provider and the Adviser that we see the unrealized value of talent intelligence. If you are stuck in the Provider delivery mechanism, even if you are making huge impact at scale, you are arguably not making the most of your talent intelligence capability. Throughout this evolution up the trust chain, it is important to ensure the following:

- Align expectations with all stakeholders as your offering is changing.

- Ensure you build the skills and capabilities within the team to deliver at the next level.

- Ensure that the quality of your work remains high. This is a key element to ensure trust is maintained and the evolution continues.

- Increase the value of the work you do. This may sound obvious but have a ruthless prioritization to ensure you really maintain focus on the high value and high impact work.

Let's dig into these a little more.

Talent intelligence provider

This involves delivering objective intelligence across customer needs, often aligned at the requisition and Sourcing Intelligence level. The work within this level will likely be clear with well-defined projects. It is likely that the majority of work will be with one team/customer. You will likely be coordinating the delivery of straightforward talent intelligence projects/ goals. Straightforward problems/efforts have minimal visible risks or roadblocks. Ambiguity is around how to implement the solution. What to accomplish is clear (and does not appear to be complicated), but how to accomplish that work is not clear. This stage defines requirements, facilitates progress, identifies blockers and increases the visibility of issues.

The work of a talent intelligence provider has moderate impact. You will be affecting team goals and project-related metrics.

Talent intelligence problem solver

This involves bringing analysis and perspective on root causes of issues identified in talent findings to help business areas take corrective action and make decisions. Whether within a company or from a vendor perspective, this can similarly be with a single customer/stakeholder but generally works across teams. Problem solvers influence their customers' talent intelligence, roadmap priorities and decisions. Although the talent intelligence strategy is likely defined, the wider business problem and solution may not be defined.

Work is tactical. You will be managing difficult and/or cross-functional talent intelligence projects/goals. This will mean difficult problems/efforts with visible risks or roadblocks, requiring skill and a considerable amount of work to resolve or deliver results. You will define talent intelligence requirements and drive team(s)/partners to meet goals. You will drive and accelerate progress by driving timely decisions. You will be able to spot risks, ask the right questions, clears blockers and escalate appropriately.

The work of a talent intelligence problem solver has a moderate impact. You will be working across multiple team goals and programme-related metrics and will likely impact a country or region.

Talent intelligence insight generator

This means taking a more proactive role in suggesting meaningful improve-ments and a talent intelligence advisory capacity. Generally, work is within and across a vice president-level organization and will influence large talent segments, workforce intelligence decisions, etc. Business problems may not be well-defined. Talent intelligence strategy may not be defined. Delivery is independent, with limited guidance.

Within this phase your work is tactical and strategic. You will own a large talent intelligence programme or account. You will be managing the full lifecycle of complex initiatives. Complex problems/efforts have visible risks, roadblocks and constraints.

The work of a talent intelligence insight generator will be high impact. You will be aligning and work across organizational level goals and programme-related metrics. Depending on the customer's footprint, you may have cross-region impact.

Talent intelligence trusted adviser

This role involves providing value-added services and proactive strategic advice to the business well beyond the effective and efficient execution of the business strategy. Business and/or workforce intelligence strategy may not be defined. It is likely that you may not even know what the problem is before starting. This adviser relationship will help drive clarity to the problems. You will work across the breadth of your organization (be this business unit or full organization depending on your own organization's power base and decision-making mechanism and set-up). You will bring a broad strategic talent intelligence influence and you will align teams and functions towards simple, coherent approaches. This role actively develops the stakeholder/customer intelligence maturity and community.

Work is strategic. You or your function will own a very large talent intelligence programme or account. You will manage significantly complex and important initiatives that resolve critical and/or endemic problems. Significantly complex problems/efforts have visible and not-yet-visible risks, roadblocks, constraints, and many conflicts with each other (i.e. resolution of one issue creates a conflict with the resolution of another issue; multiplied by the number of issues). This requires significant expertise to see around corners, make the right trade-offs and design a solution that is appropriately simple (does not add to the complexity). Due to the stakeholders involved (i.e. those blocking or driving the constraint, senior leaders, etc.) achieving alignment on an approach or implementation is more challenging and the trade-offs made usually have long-term impacts.

You will be identifying risks/opportunities in strategies and/or organizational structure(s). You will also need to make trade-offs: business opportunity versus resources versus sustainability.

The work of a talent intelligence trusted partner will be high impact. You will align to multiple organizational/customer goals and programme-related metrics. Depending on your customer base, work will likely have global impact.

Overall functional maturity model

There are a number of maturity models that overlay into the world of Talent Intelligence and align with the trusted adviser concept above.

Given our heavy data usage, the one we see most often aligned is a generic industry standard data maturity model (not to be confused with the data confidence model we discussed in Chapter 5). Although there have been a few positioned over the last 20 years they often have a similar core. This includes the following:

- Manual reporting – what has happened? Often a one-off report created with a large amount of manual intervention. With little to no analysis done and a large degree of customization and human error to be expected.

- Automated reporting – what has happened and how can we find out without as much manual intervention? This opens up time, capacity and consistency allowing a degree of analysis to come in as the reports and the associated questions (and analysis) become more standardized.

- Dashboarding – what is happening? Closer to real-time data access, cleaner data engineering and warehousing to enable a single source of truth.

- Forecasting – what will happen? With clean and consistent data sets and structured data engineering, we can finally start to forecast accurately with more confidence.

- Prediction – what will happen that we aren't looking for? At this stage of data maturity, you have the scale and clarity of data sets that means you can really look to push the boundaries with machine learning, natural language processing, automated decision support, etc.

Parallel to this data maturity model, you will often also see a broad analytics maturity model to look to get as much actionable data to the end customer as possible. This is usually via a product and self-service model. This moves from one-to-one relationships through the heavy manual intervention/ manual reporting phase to a one-to-many approach through the dashboard creating and real-time analysis, with a debate around whether one-to-all could or should be an end state with true data transparency across the organization.

We have seen this mirrored across HR analytics with a strong technical maturity and a strong product and self-service culture forming. This gives a very strong route to the customer and, as long as there is a customer analytics maturity, can enable and scale across the organization. We have seen a renaissance though in the last few years with HR analytics teams seeing specific products not landing as they would have hoped. To combat this, they have been boosting their account management/consulting mechanisms at the front end of the cycle to ensure they remain close to the customer and are building tools that are fit for purpose.

Messy scaling

One of the reasons that HR analytics are able to scale and move down this maturity path is the nature of the data they are analysing. It is usually very structured and from within their own data ecosystem, giving them a large degree of control and low(er) data ambiguity. The metrics/KPIs can be standardized, the terminology aligned and taxonomies are clean and clear.

Within Talent Intelligence, we have a slightly different dilemma. External labour market data is often far messier and unstructured. The taxonomies between vendors, government data and internal data are often ambiguous and misaligned. The external landscape is, arguably, more dynamic with more moving parts – whether that is macro, i.e. political instability, employer brand in the marketplace, tax regulations, local labour laws, trade policies, freedom of movement legislation or currency regulations, or micro, i.e. talent supply, talent demand, competitor talent movements or competitor compensation increases right through to local infrastructure. More often than not, the context for the data is as vital, if not more so, than the data point(s) in of themselves.

What does this mean in context? Let's look at some scenarios:

- Scenario 1: You are looking to expand a current site. Imagine a location analysis through a dashboard/self-service tool. Within a target commutable radius, the total talent demand, supply, cost and market penetration all look good. You have brought in the macro candidate sentiment and it all looks positive for the site and leadership. On paper this should be a strong site. But what you cannot see is that there is a toll road within that target commutable radius. This radically drops the total addressable candidate market and makes the site non-scalable without considerable efforts.

- Scenario 2: You are looking at a new location for a potential expansion. Within a target commutable radius, the total talent demand, supply and cost all look good. It is a new site, so you don't have any sentiment data, but the overall brand perception is strong. Once again this should be a strong site, however, upon further inspection the location chosen sits next to three other competitor sites that have announced their expansion plans. All offer strong compensation and career pathing and have been notorious talent magnets for your talent in the past. Now this isn't to say this will be an impossible site, but it certainly gives a context that the self-service dashboard could not show.

- Scenario 3: You are looking at your future skills development for a specific type of engineering and using the dashboard to see how this population is growing/shrinking over time. The dashboard is showing that, across the geography you are looking at, engineering is growing at a sustainable rate and there should be no reason for your function to be concerned. What the reader did not realize is that the data is using bucketed engineering taxonomies from the national labour statistics body and these bucketed taxonomies include all STEM and are not cut by the specific skills you need. This specific niche is far more nuanced and not sustainable without considerable investment.

Now of course you could certainly factor in a lot of the above context into the dashboards. You could auto-aggregate news announcements for expansions and factor that into future demand. You could build in auto alerts around skills bucketing and you could build in a map to highlight commuting hotspots or toll roads. All these are doable; but we need to be very clear about the data maturity of our customer base and the products we produce.

This messiness of labour market data means that the path to maturity, at this time, doesn't necessarily want to fit the one-to-many self-service routes for strategic decision-making. Rather, many teams are looking to adopt a maturity curve more in keeping with the trusted adviser route. They look to impact at scale by moving up in the organization and working with key decision makers to effect strategy and decisions, rather than trying to mitigate the impact of poor decisions down the road later.

Talent intelligence maturity model

So, what does this trusted adviser maturity model look like when transposed to a talent intelligence arena? Next, we will look at a potential maturity model from an experimental, foundational level of talent intelligence maturity through into a mature offering. We will consider the talent intelligence function, the focus of the work, the data you are using, the operational model and the career pathing structure within the capability.

Level 1: Experimental/Foundational

Functionally

At this initial stage, you are likely in a reactionary mode with no demand signal of upcoming workloads. Capacity management is very difficult due to the lack of demand signal. Workload is largely task related and you have limited exposure to the overall context to the work and overall strategy.

Work focus

Your work focus is likely looking at 0–6 months decision-point work coupled with deep dives for unforeseen circumstances. This is highly erratic work and you will likely be pulled into the latest 'fire' to put it out. This is a fantastic period for experimenting with potential customers to see the type of work that they may find interesting as you build and stabilize.

Data

From a data perspective, you have little in place concerning data governance or engineering. You are likely at the early stages of buying your tooling with little data maturity within your stakeholder group.

Operationally

You will likely have no vision, mission, KPIs, customer definition, systems or processes in place, meaning that tracking, monitoring and scaling is challenging.

Career pathing

At this stage, you will likely be deciding between talent intelligence as a capability versus Talent Intelligence as a function. Career pathing is confused and likely to be very ill-defined. You will likely have no specialization at this time.

Level 2: Tactical

Functionally

You are starting to have closer customer alignment. This is giving you a cleaner demand signal for work. You are also leveraging the operational structures you have put in place to ensure clean work prioritization. You likely largely still work in isolation but with some engagement with other functions across the organization to ensure alignment, be it HR, finance, real estate, intelligence, etc.

Work focus

Your work focus is likely looking at 0–12 months decision-point work, coupled with deep dives for unforeseen circumstances. This is starting to see more impact in the decision-making cycle, but with a strong tactical element.

Data

You will have a somewhat standardized data structure and product offering. You will understand the limitations of your data sets.

Operationally

You will have your vision, mission, KPIs, customer definition, systems and processes in place meaning tracking, monitoring and scaling are becoming more feasible.

Career pathing

Career pathing is starting to become clearer; you will start to see role definition and specialization within the team but it is unlikely that there will be development paths in place.

Level 3: Operational

Functionally

You have very strong customer alignment and account management giving you a clean demand signal for work. Although you are leveraging the operational structures you have put in place to ensure clean work prioritization, due to the closer customer alignment you are able to get ahead of the work more. Capacity loading is less of an issue and work prioritization is happening in conjunction with your customer base. You will start to work closer with other functions across the organization to ensure alignment such as HR, finance, real estate, intelligence, etc.

Work focus

Your work focus is likely looking at 3–18 months decision-point work, coupled with deep dives for unforeseen circumstances. This is strong, impactful work that is affecting decisions made across your business. You will be aligned to core strategic goals and working with senior leadership.

Data

You will have a standardized data structure and product offering. You will understand the limitations of your data sets and look to augment this with alternative data sets, both externally and internally.

Operationally

Due to the robust systems, processes, tools and KPIs in place, you can clearly articulate your measurable business impact value. This gives you the business case to look to scale across the organization and customer base at an increased rate.

Career pathing

Career pathing is clear, with structured development paths in place across the majority of your role specializations.

Level 4: Strategic

Functionally

Very strong customer relationships; you are seen as true talent intelligence partners. Capacity loading is not an issue with close leadership alignment and work prioritization happening in conjunction with your customer base. You will see more and more collaboration with other functions across the organization to ensure alignment, such as with HR, finance, real estate, intelligence, etc.

Work focus

Your work focus is likely looking at 3–18 months-plus decision-point work, coupled with longer term vision and strategy alignment. This is strong, strategically impactful work, impacting your customer base as a whole in their longer-term strategic vision.

Data

Having understood the limitations of your data sets, you have augmented this with a larger number of data sets both externally and internally. You start to expand the data sets beyond HR and talent data to also look at real estate, infrastructure, political stability, ease of doing business, etc.

Operationally

You have very clean processes in place to enable rapid scaling and can be flexible to customer needs and changes in the model.

Career pathing

Career pathing is clear, with structured development paths in place and you should be a talent magnet for teams internally and externally.

Level 5: Transformational

Functionally

You are a talent intelligence trusted adviser across your organization. You may be centralized as a team, but you are truly embedded within your customer's organization. Capacity management is not an issue. You have true alignment to the long-term business strategy and can help guide and challenge this. You work closely with other functions across the organization to ensure alignment, such as HR, finance, real estate, intelligence, etc.

Work focus

Your work focus is likely looking at 18 months-plus longer term vision and strategy work. You are fundamentally challenging the business on their strategy, their model, the market and their positioning.

Data

You have a clean and consistent data offering in place, offering a pan-silo holistic data set. The data engineering means you can scale at will while offering truly contextual intelligence.

Operationally

All systems, processes and tools are in place and work as a well-oiled machine.

Career pathing

You have clear development paths in place across all roles and at all levels and are widely recognized as having best in class career pathing.

Summary

Building out a new functionality, especially one that has such a large degree of trust involved, is not a quick process. But it is important to remember that it is possible to fast-track elements of this maturity model and hit certain milestones ahead of time. You may have a strategic data governance in place while output as a team is still operational, for example.

In the beginning, it will feel like you are spread too thinly. You will feel like you lack alignment and focus and are too scrappy. This is perfectly normal. Take the time at the beginning to look to experiment with customers with 'pilots' to see what work is feasible, repeatable and if need be scalable and be clear about what that would mean capacity wise.

This maturity model provides some guiding principles, but it is important to identify your own north star and your own guiding light to give you and your function direction. Your maturity model may take you in a different direction. This is all new ground. Do not be afraid to deviate off the more obvious path and explore the edges.

TOBY'S TAKEAWAYS

- 'A jack-of-all-trades is a master of none, but oftentimes better than a master of one.' Know it is very normal to feel stretched too thin and that you are failing in the early days when you are having to run multiple project types across stakeholders and are very scrappy. This is the moment to experiment and play with the offering.

- We are all on this journey together. Different teams will be at different stages and no one has mastered this yet.

- You should use this maturity model as a framework but build your own version for your own north star.

- It is really hard to be a trusted adviser to a business leader. Trust takes time to build over time, consistency and output. Do not try to force it.

09

Tooling and resources

Starting out in the world of talent intelligence can feel overwhelming. With dozens of new platforms, systems, processes and tooling, along with hundreds of data sources all dispersed across the web, where do you start? The good news is that it does not need to feel overwhelming and that you likely have access to many tools and resources that will give you the kick-start needed to get your talent intelligence offering off the ground.

Let us start off by looking at some of the internal resources that may be available to you.

Internal tooling and resources

As previously discussed, often talent intelligence capabilities are situated in one of the many HR functions. Internal HR systems and sources can be a goldmine for any team looking to flex their talent intelligence muscle. This includes your Human Capital Management (HCM), Applicant Tracking System (ATS), Candidate Resource Management (CRM) solutions, as well as any other software managing compensation and benefits, talent management or anything HR analytics gets to play with. Along with this, you can also find rich data sets in finance, marketing intelligence, real estate or cyber security, to name a few. Most organizations carry large amounts of data, but it's often siloed and poorly shared. This is the time to look to build relationships and bridges company-wide to leverage data more holistically.

Human Capital Management (HCM)

Your HCM system, you may also call it a Human Resources Information System (HRIS), is a tool that enables companies to manage their workforce better. It is a holistic suite of applications that can cover everything from recruiting, onboarding, absence management, e-learning, performance management, payroll or compensation. If people are our biggest asset, then your HCM is your asset management system. Data within could range from recruitment application date, onboarding date, training completed, any information within a talent card, performance review data, any performance feedback data, organization structures, levelling, tenure, goals, job family, location, etc.

There are a number of large HCM vendors including Workday, Oracle, UKG (Ultimate Kronos Group), Cornerstone on Demand or SAP SuccessFactors HCM; but there are dozens of excellent platforms out there in this dynamic market.

The joy of HCM systems for talent intelligence is that if your company is using all the facets of these platforms you should, in theory, be able to get a very clean 'apply to leave' candidate and employee journey. This offers a unique and holistic view of the entire candidate and employee lifecycle. In reality, this is rarely the case, with often a lot of data friction between the various platform products and often entire products not enabled with other 'best in class' tooling preferred and integrated.

Nevertheless, the potential for data use for talent intelligence using HCM data is huge. Depending if you have an HR analytics capability or not, you could start with simple questions such as:

- What source of hire do we find most of our top performers come from?

- How does employee engagement correlate with our attrition rate or time to hire?

- What target company candidates have the most success through our recruiting funnel?

- How does training rate effect attrition?

You can then look to evolve by pulling in external data to augment this (sources to be discussed later in this chapter) to questions such as:

- How does our employee engagement correlate with our external candidate sentiment?

- How does candidate perception impact our recruiting funnel?

- What percentage of the market have we already exhausted from a talent perspective and how does this affect future viability?

- How does our compensation philosophy affect our candidate pipeline and how does this compare to our competitors?
- How does our span of control within the organization effect attrition and how does this compare to the market?

Applicant Tracking System (ATS)

The ATS is a specialized system for your recruitment tracking needs. This is often rolled into a larger HCM suite but many Talent Acquisition teams will look to have a specialized and dedicated ATS that may or may not align and integrate into the broader HCM.

Some of the largest ATS systems are iCIMS, Jobvite, SmartRecruiters, Ceridian, Greenhouse and Bullhorn, along with the specific recruitment modules of the HCM platforms mentioned earlier: UKG Ready Recruiting, Workday Recruiting, SAP SuccessFactors Recruiting and Oracle Recruiting Cloud.

Similarly, to the HCM the data within the ATS is incredibly rich and useful to help pose some initial questions for any talent intelligence team, such as:

- What roles take the longest to hire?
- What locations have abnormally high time to hire?
- What companies do we have high success hiring from?
- Where can we see un-natural fallout through our recruitment funnel?

Once again, these more traditional TA Analytics questions can then be enriched with a talent intelligence mindset.

- Do we have a diverse representation of the market applying for roles?
- How are competitor X's hiring strategies affecting our talent funnel?
- How is our role levelling versus the market impacting our talent attraction and funnel conversion?
- How is our candidate perception affecting our channel conversion?

Most ATS systems have been designed role first, i.e. they will sort and track candidates against the roles that have been created. This means there is often no space for speculative candidate applications and searching across the platform is not a core activity it has been designed for. This means that often companies will look to also have a candidate relationship management system as well as their ATS to look to track and monitor candidates more effectively.

Candidate Relationship Management (CRM)

As the name suggests, unlike the ATS, the CRM has the candidate at its core. The CRM has been designed to target the early stage of the recruitment funnel – often with a strong recruitment marketing component (growing in maturity rapidly). It can be used for awareness, interest, nurturing and engagement in those early stages before a candidate looks to apply to a specific role. The whole system is designed around tracking and engaging with candidates. If your market is very company-driven, with a high application rate and your adverts are your primary source of hire, then you may just need the ATS. But if your market is more candidate-driven, and you need to do more proactive search, outreach and engagement, then you may also look to a CRM to support this activity.

The data within a CRM is complementary to that within the ATS, but can also offer fresh insight. You could look at questions such as:

- What is our success rate targeting candidates from competitor X?
- How many times do we need to engage with a candidate before they want to apply to a role with us?
- What days do we see the greatest prospect engagement?

Once again, you can take a talent intelligence slant on this data:

- How does our share price affect our prospect outreach success rate?
- How can we capture all sourcing intelligence data at scale to use for macro talent intelligence?
- How does competitor lay-off news translate to our prospect outreach success?

External resources

As well as the wealth of internal resources and data sources, there are a lot of resources available to you externally. Some of these will be curated, some raw data sets, some platforms and some relationship- and partner-based.

This is a new field and there is little standardization around how this landscape should work together yet. With this in mind, be creative and explore the sources and relationships to create what you need as appropriate for your organization.

Vendors

Look to explore your external relationships with labour market providers. This includes job boards, recruitment process outsourcing firms, research firms, competitor intelligence firms, consulting organizations, recruitment firms, master managed agencies or even payroll providers, as they will all likely have access to large amounts of primary data. It is likely that some or all of these partners will be looking at ways to explore their data sets and to help support their customers. It is equally likely that this is still new to them and they would look to explore co-creation and development with you as a customer.

Be open and transparent with your needs and where the benefit for them as a vendor could be. It is often the case that even if they are exploring this space, they may not have any mechanisms in place as to how to facilitate any knowledge sharing or how to price this into a contract or relationship. Explore the options, explore the data together and see what can be built.

External platforms

As you look to develop your talent intelligence capabilities, it is likely that you will need to augment your internal data with some external data sources. One of the first steps for most is to look at an aggregated external data platform such as Stratigens, Talent Neuron, LinkedIn Talent Insights, Horsefly Analytics, EMSI Burning Glass, Draup or Claro.

Depending on the platform you will see various options and models:

- some are just the platform
- some have support reports and workbenches
- some have libraries of previous research completed
- some will aggregate broader data sets than just labour market
- some are stock off the shelf and some are fully customizable
- some are driven from candidate profiles
- some from macro government data

The options are seemingly endless. What you pick, and most importantly what combination you pick, will largely be driven by your use cases internally, your user base (specific Talent Intelligence individuals versus all of Talent Acquisition for example), the geographies you want to cover and your price point.

Given the range of products I would always look to partner two vendors together to then compare and validate with a third external data source. This is a common data triangulation methodology, whereby directional data can be corroborated and any weaknesses in the various data sets can be compensated for by the strengths of other data from the other sources, thereby increasing the validity and the reliability of the results overall. It is worth recognizing this is not a perfect science; you will find challenges with the data (to be discussed in integration challenges later) and you really need to be clear on data refresh rates on your sources to be able to ensure you have a clear picture of what you are looking at.

I will not dive deeply into each of the vendors, as their offerings are changing and improving daily and I would not want to do them a disservice. I did though want to say a few words around LinkedIn given its positioning and industry penetration.

LinkedIn

LinkedIn is the one system that stands slightly alone in the traditional suite of products given their penetration into the talent acquisition landscape, with many using this as a parallel CRM to their inhouse system. Their main product offerings are Talent Solutions, Marketing Solutions, Sales Solutions and Learning Solutions; it could be argued that this is the beginning of a highly dynamic HCM suite. Within this context LinkedIn offers two main products of interest for interest to Talent Intelligence teams, LinkedIn Recruiter and LinkedIn Talent Insights, both sitting within Talent Solutions.

For this conversation, we will focus in on Talent Solutions and the main products within LinkedIn Recruiter and LinkedIn Talent Insights (LTI). LinkedIn Recruiter is a back-end product that enables much of the features you would see within an ATS or CRM but with the dynamic data set of the LinkedIn membership base on the front end. This gives a unique product and offering that is one of the key tools within many Talent Acquisition teams armoury. To try to reduce platform fatigue LinkedIn have partnered with a number of ATS vendors such as Bullhorn, Greenhouse, Jobvite, iCIMS, JobDiva, Lever, Oracle, Workday or Workable, among others, to integrate into their offerings and position themselves as a dynamic CRM front-end platform.

Although LinkedIn Recruiter is not a talent intelligence product, as we discussed in Chapter 5 there are a number of elements within that are highly valuable for any talent intelligence efforts. These include but are not limited to: the Total Accessible Market (note not total Addressable market as that would include everyone off platform, this name better reflects the immediately accessible talent pool within LinkedIn); the location of the talent; the key competitors for this talent; the education history of these candidates; and the historical companies of these candidates. These are all very useful for both sourcing intelligence and Talent Intelligence activities.

LinkedIn Talent Insights (LTI) is LinkedIn's foray into the world of talent intelligence. Unlike all other platforms, it uses only the LinkedIn data set and does not look to cross reference with any external data sets. There are pros and cons to this. In countries with low LinkedIn market penetration, the variance between the platform figures and those from other vendors looking at multiple data sets can be wide. The real benefit is that the data points users will see within LTI are very similar to those they will see in LIR (for better or for worse). This means that you see a large comfort level with recruiters using the tool (along with a very familiar LinkedIn user interface) where they feel confident in the numbers being presented as it feels similar to what they are seeing in LIR. This can increase product uptake but, when you are looking at making big decisions rather than sourcing feasibility, you need to be very conscious, as with all platforms, about what the data is showing you versus the actual market, especially in those regions, job functions and industries with low LinkedIn penetration rate.

Macro data sets

There are many macro-economic labour market data set sources that are available and usually free to use. These include the International Labour Organization, the US Bureau of Labor Statistics, OECD Skills for Jobs, Eurostat, World Bank, CIA World Factbook and EU Open Data Portal, to name but a few.

These macro data sets can be invaluable to any Talent Intelligence team to really see the context of the data points they are looking at from a macro perspective. For example, if you are looking at gender diversity rates in a given job family, in a location using one of the external platforms mentioned previously, it would be largely meaningless without understanding the contextual labour force participation rate overall in that location. They can also be of huge value if you are looking to build out a Talent Intelligence Futurist capability to look ahead into the future and predict headwinds from a macroeconomic perspective. These could be questions such as: how will changes in labour force participation rates affect our ability to staff up our organization? How will historical and current higher education levels impact our early careers programme feasibility in the next three to five years? How will a country's demographics and baby boomer retiree rate affect our organization and associated knowledge transfer? How will historical, current, and projected international migration rates effect our ability to staff up our organization?

These are large, broad and highly complex and contextual questions and topics but are vital to set the broader economic and socio-economic context for your work.

Targeted local bodies

After these large macro data sets, you can start to target more specific local statistical, governmental or financial bodies. These are numerous and varied, depending on the specific country you are trying to target, but some examples are: Statistics Poland, Hungarian Central Statistical Office, Statistics Slovakia, China Statistics, Beijing Statistics, Czech Statistical Office, the central bank of any given country, ministries of finance, ministries of labour, ministries of tourism, ministries of trade, etc.

It is important to remember that these bodies will usually come with a specific view or agenda, so although their data is credible it needs to be seen in the context of their perspective. Each government, state or local municipality that has a trade or 'invest in' programme will naturally want to put the data for their location in the best possible light. This is not to say it is not valid or reliable; you just need to ensure the methodology is robust and the context for the data is understood.

SEC filings

One area that is of growing interest is that of SEC filings. The SEC is the Securities and Exchange Commission (SEC), which is an independent agency of the United States federal government whose primary purpose is to enforce the law against market manipulation. In late 2020, they adopted amendments to Items 101, 103 and 105 of Regulation S-K. These amendments added human capital resources as a disclosure topic under Item 101. The SEC did not specify what their definition of human capital resources meant, nor did they specify what metrics or measures they would require companies to report on, which led to some widespread criticism of the guidelines. However, we have now seen the first wave of filings under the new guidelines and we can see some themes coming through.

Some of the topics that are appearing so far, to varying degrees of depth of disclosure, are:

- diversity and inclusion
- talent development/learning and development
- succession planning
- compensation and benefits
- talent attraction and retention
- employee split between full time and part time
- unionization and employee relations
- employee health and wellbeing
- organizational culture/employee engagement

The depth and quality of the reporting was varied: some more quantitative and some more qualitative; some mentioned in passing; some highly explicit and detailed. These are still the early days for the filings, but the power and potential from a talent intelligence perspective is huge. We look forward to seeing how this develops over time with increased investor scrutiny and refinement of disclosures.

A list of resources that I and the Talent Intelligence Collective have pulled together in the past, from platforms, podcasts, government bodies and so on, can be found here: www.koganpage.com/talent-intelligence (archived at https://perma.cc/XFZ7-3AAC).

Integration challenges

Data quality/validity/taxonomies

Most talent intelligence offerings look to cover very similar parameters within their studies. These will often be parameters such as:

- talent flows
- labour pool supply
- labour pool demand
- labour cost
- university graduates
- labour pipeline
- quality of life
- political stability
- ease of doing business
- labour market efficiency
- organization attractiveness

The challenges come when comparing data sets across platforms/vendors/ sources and across geographies. Between platforms and sources, the main challenge is around data definitions/normalization. How is each source defining the parameter you are looking at? For example, if you are looking at the talent availability of software engineers in a given city you may have to consider the following:

- How is the platform defining 'software engineer'? Is it using the exact phrase versus fuzzy logic to imply that someone is a software engineer given other parameters?
- How are they defining the city? Is itself a reported location? Is it a greater metropolitan area?
- Are they driving the results by job title categorization or by skills categorization?
- What data sources are they using for their platform and what are the associated data limitations?
- How do the assumptions around title levelling or scope compare to your internal data? Is your software development engineer equal to the same titled role in another company or is it higher or lower levelled? Is there a broader or narrower scope? Are you all looking for equivalent experience levels?
- How do your titles compare across markets and potentially languages and is that picked up by your vendor?
- What is the data refresh rate for the sources you are looking at?

Now, the good news is there are movements to bring standardization to at least the job and skills taxonomy side of things with both the O*NET-SOC (Standard Occupational Classification) Taxonomy and the EMSI Open Skills Taxonomy open access to all. With this standardization and clarity, the quality of data and ease of access to the data from an end user experience will increase considerably.

Summary

As we can see, the talent intelligence data landscape is still very contextual and subjective, but there are lots of tools and resources available. Do not feel like you immediately need to have a plethora of tooling or a small army of headcount and specialists to build out a talent intelligence capability. There are lots of internal resources available; lots of teams that would be open to partnership; lots of external data sets available to investigate for free. Certainly you will want to invest, specialize and develop as you mature but do not let this be a barrier to entry to the world of Talent Intelligence for you or your organization.

TOBY'S TAKEAWAYS

- There will be opportunities to co-create and explore partnerships across your organization. Be open-minded and think big about the power and potential for talent data.

- Do not worry about siloed responsibilities: talent intelligence is most powerful in a pan silo collaborative environment.

- Be conscious of data sources and data quality. Be aware of what the data is telling you and also what is not available within it.

- Be deliberate about your data source choices to maximize strengths and minimize weaknesses of your tool architecture as a whole, by complementary tooling and platforms.

- This is an ongoing moving topic. Keep abreast of the data landscape and changes and how they will affect your talent intelligence offering.

10

Potential structures of talent intelligence teams

Since time immemorial, humans have looked to work collaboratively and in ever-increasingly efficient ways. Since the industrial revolution this has really increased with organizations wrestling with optimal organizational design and functional design to allow optimal performance of the workforce and organization. This is an ongoing issue that organizations wrestle with and is something you will likely wrestle with when setting up and building out your talent intelligence capabilities.

Broadly speaking, we see four main structures of dedicated talent intelligence functions: business unit aligned, geographical market aligned, functional alignment and product offering aligned. Each will have their pros and cons and which you choose should largely be driven by how the power base and decision-making power sits within your organization.

Business unit aligned

Business unit alignment is often used in decentralized organizations with highly autonomous business units or divisions. From a talent intelligence perspective, this enables you to be close to the customer, move fast and be very targeted and aware from a competitor intelligence and business-specific skills intelligence perspective. It can, though, leave you exposed with a lack of group functional intelligence expertise, a lack of geographic coverage in areas where your business does not have a footprint or a lack of depth of product if your business area does not have a demand for that product offering.

Geographical market aligned

Geographical market alignment is often used in decentralized organizations with highly autonomous geographical markets. From a talent intelligence perspective, this enables you to be close to the customer, move fast and be very targeted and aware from a regional location intelligence perspective, with all the nuances that can bring, understanding the key competitors in the region and really understanding the regionally-specific talent and skills intelligence. It can, though, leave you exposed with a lack of group functional intelligence expertise, a lack of broader, business unit level competitor intelligence or a lack of depth of product if your geographic or market area leadership do not have a demand for a given product offering.

Functional alignment

Functional alignment is often used in centralized organizations with a high degree of control coming from the central body. From a talent intelligence perspective, this enables you to see things at a macro and holistic level across the organization. This can lead to better control of resources, vision on future skills gaps and better alignment on functional strategies, be it organizational design, role design or location strategies. It can, though, leave you exposed with a lack of business or commercial competitor intelligence expertise, a lack of geographic or regional market intelligence or a lack of depth of product if your functional leadership do not have a demand for a given product offering.

Product offering aligned

Product alignment is one of the most powerful organizational designs, but it can leave you exposed. This is where you would align the team around specific product offerings, be it location intelligence, competitor intelligence, candidate intelligence, organizational benchmarking, etc. From a talent intelligence perspective, this enables you to have a large degree of specialization and a deep expertise in given product areas which leads to a more robust and higher quality output product for the end customer. However, this does come at a price: teams with product alignment can find it hard to get close enough to a customer group (be it business unit, function or market) as interactions are often piecemeal. Individuals within the teams can also suffer from output fatigue – doing the same types of studies so frequently can lead to dissatisfaction and team attrition. This also exposes a challenge with this model, as there is less product exposure across the team, so you have single points of failure with little capacity to manage if people leave.

There will likely be missed opportunities for all these models, so a fifth option is available – albeit harder to align as a team. This is the hybrid model.

Hybrid matrix model

This model takes elements of each of the above to try to align in alliance to the company power base primarily, then with a second overlay alignment to look at maximizing opportunities. This looks to maximize the opportunity presented through traditional business-as-usual mechanisms and decision-making, while keeping the specialization and deep subject matter expertise, be it product, market or business unit.

This can be done by having individuals multi-hat, e.g. someone could both be the talent intelligence subject matter expert for competitor intelligence, plus an expert in their market, or an expert in location strategy and also deeply embedded in their account or business unit. This multi-hat arrangement can be hugely powerful and allows for deep knowledge but with variety of work maintained. It can lead to challenges as you look to grow and mature though, as individuals can feel like they are not fulfilling either of their hats to their full potential.

Another hybrid model is to look to have the core relationship/account management in a very defined split (be it market, business unit, product or function), but then have specialist talent intelligence areas running across all accounts in a pan function capacity. For example, you could have account managers aligned by market – they build all relationships across the market leadership and they are the deep-seated subject matter experts in the regional market labour market context. But then you may have specializations such as competitor intelligence, DEI intelligence or software market intelligence running across all markets in pan team support. For example, if your organization is led and driven by market/region, it may look like Figure 10.1.

FIGURE 10.1   Pan team support across markets/regions

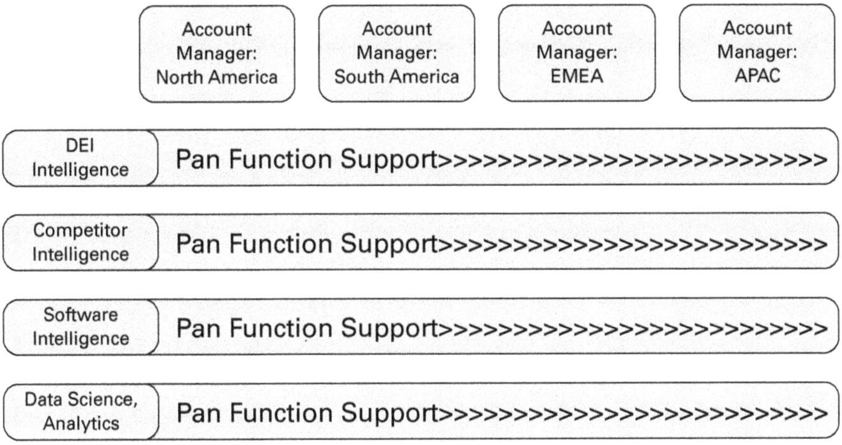

Or, if your organization is driven by a business unit model with operations in Europe, Middle East, Africa and Asia Pacific, it may look like Figure 10.2.

FIGURE 10.2   Pan team support by business unit model

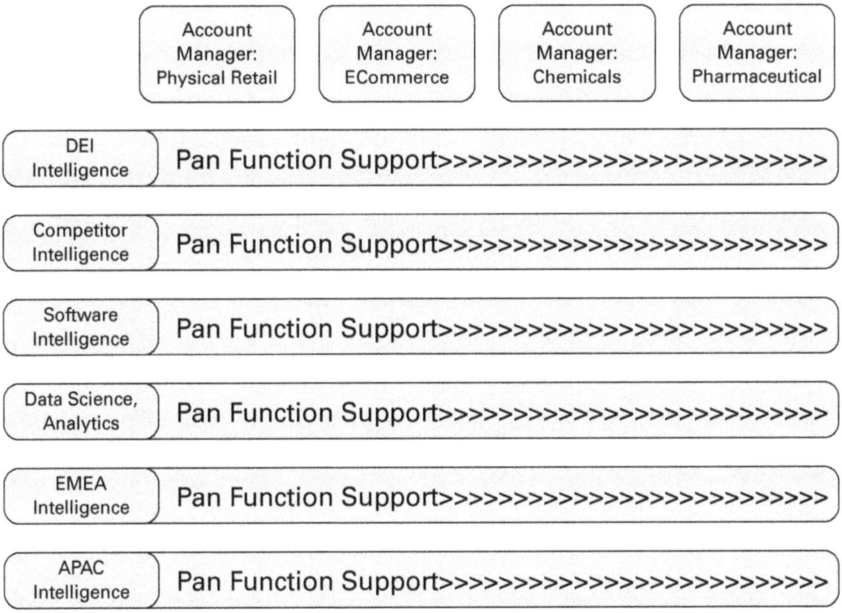

Centralized versus de-centralized

Within all of these models – business unit, market, functional or hybrid – you also have the option to be a centralized or decentralized talent intelligence function.

Centralized

The centralized talent intelligence team means that all the members of the talent intelligence function are managed directly within the centralized talent intelligence team, regardless of whether they are aligned to business areas, markets or functions.

The major benefits to this approach include the following:

- Given the consolidated holistic view, a centralized team can prioritize across all work over the company.
- Tighter cohesion among the talent intelligence team members in a single team and community with a single focused vision and mission that the team can align behind.
- Less resistance and fewer roadblocks with knowledge sharing and a greater ability for peer-to-peer learning and support.
- More flexibility and fluidity with respect to capacity management with the ability to move talent intelligence resources onto projects that need temporary help.
- Arguably more career path opportunities as the centralized scale offers specialization and management career path routes that would be far harder to scale in a decentralized model.
- Economies of scale and reduced cost. With centralized systems, processes, tooling and resource management, you reduce duplication of workload, reduce waste within the process and reduce duplicative responsibilities due to simplified chain of command.
- Standardized and consistent output of work across all customer bases.

However, with centralization teams you can equally have the following:

- increased layers of leadership and associated bureaucracy
- delays in work, as there will be an increase in process and an increase in decision-making

- often decision makers are further from the customer so the end customer can struggle to feel like they are able to move fast or effectively
- output is often standardized and not specific to customer needs

Decentralized

A decentralized talent intelligence team means that all the members of the talent intelligence function are managed locally and embedded within the business unit, market or function with those talent intelligence functions often having very little knowledge of or interaction with talent intelligence individuals/teams from other parts of the company. The benefits of this approach can be inferred by looking at the disadvantages of the approach above, but can be summarized with the following:

- talent intelligence members/teams being directly embedded in the planning and execution of work for each team locally
- each team has dedicated talent intelligence resources to use as they see fit
- reduced layers of leadership and associated bureaucracy
- a clear focus on the vision and mission of the business unit/market/function that they are aligned to, meaning that they can have clear line of sight for all work and how it impacts their area
- talent intelligence individuals who work for any given team learn about that team's mission and require no additional ramp-up or onboarding time when they start a new project
- rapid delivery in work, as there will be less process and fewer associated decision-making steps
- decision makers are embedded with the customer so they are able to move fast and effectively
- output is often non-standardized and customized, specific to customer needs
- greater opportunity for pan function learning and development and parallel career pathing

However, with decentralization teams you can equally have:

- fewer career options within the team due to the smaller size and scale
- fewer economies in scale leading to reduced capacity, tooling and investment and increased cost

- fewer opportunities for peer-to-peer learning and knowledge management and transfer
- less standardization, leading to confusion in output between customer groups

Centralized ringfenced

The third option is centralized ringfencing. This option looks to take the benefits of scale centralization and the autonomy and speed, local knowledge and embedded nature of decentralization. With this model you have teams/individuals whose headcount and reporting structure is centralized but who are ringfenced and aligned to specific business units/market/functions/products. This gives you the career pathing, efficiency, peer learning, support structure, holistic view and capacity management and flexibility of a centralized team but importantly by being ringfenced and aligned it means that individuals have the flexibility, specialization and relationships at a local level to move fast and impact the customer directly.

There is, of course, one important factor within talent intelligence that many traditional models of organizational and workload design and effectiveness do not fully account for and that is the fact talent intelligence has knowledge management rather than purely product output at its core.

Knowledge management

As highlighted, Knowledge Management (KM) is at the core of any intelligence function and that is true of talent intelligence also. The knowledge management process is often summarized as involving knowledge acquisition, creation, refinement, storage, transfer, sharing and utilization.

Within this we can essentially look at three core steps of knowledge acquisition or creation, storage and sharing/dissemination. It is often easy to focus on the acquisition of knowledge, be it through your own research or through finding other research of value. This naturally aligns with a process workflow and will happen very naturally as you start to build your talent intelligence muscle. Too many though stop at this level. They create projects and deliver these to the customer or stakeholders and do not think about how this data should be stored or shared in the future in a scalable way. I would implore you to build a saleable and repeatable process around this though. Think through the following questions:

- Where is appropriate to store this research? Are third-party vendors even an option if you are storing corporately sensitive material?
- Who will be looking to use this research later? What is their data retrieval comfort level?
- How will you enable them to search for this research? Is it through structured filing structures? Is it through a purpose-built knowledge or content management tool?
- What is safe to store in this repository – everything? Only projects deemed unclassified or unrestricted?
- Do you want data partitioning by user type?
- Do you want search functionality or filtering?

Once you have this in place, you should then also think about how this information is shared across your target groups. This is where your communications strategy, as we discussed in Chapter 6, will come into play to have targeted intelligence communications proactively out from your team, but also it will be vital to build a culture of knowledge sharing from within your core user groups (traditionally Talent Intelligence, Talent Acquisition, Executive Recruitment and broader HR, but you could absolutely extend this to the broader business stakeholders too). This human involvement and cultural element cannot be under-emphasized. You need to start from the leadership and look to drive a culture that rewards and empowers a knowledge-sharing culture. Look to also have knowledge sharing champions across your partner teams that will act as local subject matter experts and facilitate learning of the knowledge management tool and help drive the knowledge and intelligence culture.

Team size

I am often asked how big a Talent Intelligence function needs to be. This is an impossible question to answer, as it will largely depend on your customer base, your geographic spread, your complexity and your service offering. As a guide, in the 2021 Talent Intelligence Collective Benchmarking Survey, nearly 70 per cent of all respondents highlighted that they had a ratio of 1 team member for up to every 50 customers/stakeholders.[1]

Remember, for this to be true you need to be clear and intentional about who the true customer is. If you are supporting an organization of 5000, but you only engage with the top 1 per cent of leaders, then be clear about your actual customer base of 50 versus 5000. But equally, if your stakeholders are high-level decision makers you could quite feasibly look to have a 1:1 or 1:2 relationship with a senior Talent Intelligence Trusted Adviser aligning with your senior leaders to be their strategic talent advisers. The engagement level and capacity truly need to be whatever is appropriate for your organization and the model you look to follow.

Summary

So, what is the right model? As much as possible I would recommend aligning to this power base so, for example, if your business is driven by business units, align accordingly. If it is driven by market, align accordingly. If functionally, align accordingly, etc. I would then consider the centralized ringfenced overlay, e.g. a centralized team that is aligned by market, a centralized team that is aligned by business unit, a centralized team that is aligned by function or a centralized function aligned by product area. Essentially, though, it is important to start with the end customer, their needs, the desired relationship and the desired output, then work backwards from there.

TOBY'S TAKEAWAYS

- Look to reflect the business and customer power base in your team alignment.
- Be open to models and be conscious this will change and flex as your function matures, specializes and the business models change.
- Look to maximize capacity by supporting pan silo with work that is repeatable across the accounts and customer groups.
- Do not ignore knowledge management and knowledge sharing. Build the culture of knowledge sharing from the top.

Endnote

1 The Talent Intelligence Collective 2021 Benchmarking Survey. See resources from the Talent Intelligence Collective at: www.koganpage.com/talent-intelligence (archived at https://perma.cc/XFZ7-3AAC).

11

Roles and skills needed in teams

As we are finding out, the talent intelligence space is still evolving. As such, the roles, skills and capabilities needed within the team are still broad and at times ill-defined. In this chapter we are going to explore this in a little more detail looking at the current state and future state of what is needed from a skill, competency and role perspective in a multidisciplinary talent intelligence capability.

For the purpose of this chapter, we will define roles, skills and capabilities as follows:

- Skills: granular, specific activities that are needed to complete your role. They are tactical in nature and are often repeated frequently in order to complete a task.
- Competencies: strategically important and will align to and help drive overall business or functional impact.
- Roles: specific headcount with defined responsibilities around a specific deliverable.

Skills

The 2021 Talent Intelligence Collective Benchmarking Survey asked respondents what top five skills they are looking to develop, maintain or remove from their function in 2022. The findings from this were telling in the context of the respondent's current work focus, their desired future state and the breadth of the skills gap they are faced with. You could argue that some of the below are actually competencies rather than skills, but this is what the survey found.

Skills to maintain

Overall, the top five skills that respondents wanted to maintain, suggesting currently in place, throughout 2022 were: Sourcing (64.7 per cent), Project Management (52.9 per cent), Problem Solving (49 per cent), Stakeholder Management (47 per cent) and Workforce Planning (39.2 per cent). From this we can see that sourcing is still seen as a core skill set needed by the majority of Talent Intelligence teams. This aligns with 50 per cent of the respondents highlighting that Sourcing or Talent Mapping are their top priorities followed by location strategy, Diversity and Competitor Intelligence. If you look across the remaining skills, they are a mix of hard and soft skills – albeit soft skills (stakeholder management or problem solving) that can be trained and developed through technical training, process and structure. Overall, though, these are all skills closely aligned with sourcing intelligence and the more consultative side of talent intelligence.

Skills to develop

Overall, the top five skills that respondents wanted to develop, suggesting not currently in place but an important focus area throughout 2022 and beyond, were: Data Visualization (80.4 per cent), Predictive Analytics (78.4 per cent), Data Analysis (74.5 per cent), Strategic Consulting (68.6 per cent), Machine Learning (68.6 per cent) and Data Engineering (62.75 per cent). When we look at the skills that people want to develop, we see a very strong message that teams feel they need to improve their hard skilled, technical data capabilities whether in visualization, analysis or engineering with the one non-technical skill being that of strategic consulting. Overall, we can see that teams are looking to up-level their work and give their consulting individuals the data foundations to be able to consult at a strategically impactful level.

Skills to remove

Overall, the top five skills that respondents wanted to remove, suggesting currently in place but not a focus area for 2022 or beyond were: Sourcing (15.7 per cent), Workforce Planning (11.7 per cent), Machine Learning (11.7 per cent), Data Engineering (11.76 per cent) and Predictive Analytics (7.8 per cent). It is interesting, given the prominence of sourcing and talent mapping in the current state, that the number one skill set that teams wanted to remove was Sourcing. This suggests that, although it is still central to many teams, this is not a service offering that people see as a core deliverable moving forward. It is surprising to see some of the more technical skills in Machine Learning, Data Engineering and Predictive Analytics being in this list. This would suggest that these skills are in place within teams but not being utilized fully currently. My theory around this is that few teams have the data architecture in place and the level of data engineering or data quality to truly look towards building out predictive analytics or machine learning within a talent intelligence capability. These skills are still relatively new in the more stable and structured world of HR Analytics and to adopt this across talent intelligence in the far messier and unstructured data sets is incredibly challenging.

Competencies

Competencies are a set of characteristics that enable and improve the efficiency or performance of a job. They are strategically important and will align to and help drive overall business or functional impact. These are not granular and specific skill sets, but larger characteristics that will drive the culture of your team and ability to align with and deliver against business goals.

There will be numerous competencies that you will need to drive within your specific version of talent intelligence within your firm, but I would argue that there are a number of competencies that are at the heart of most Talent Intelligence teams. Let's dig into these in a little more detail.

Problem solving

Being able to both define a problem, identify the root cause of this problem, then work through to identify potential solutions is core to any TI capability. This problem-solving competence is frequently cited as one of the key skills required in the ambiguous and changing future we face and yet it is surprisingly hard to find in the workplace. Given the types of questions we face in talent intelligence and the structured process we need to follow to effectively deliver our solutions, a core problem solving skill set and inquisitive nature will be absolutely key today and in the future.

Critical thinking

There are several definitions for critical thinking but within a TI context I would say it is the ability to observe, analyse, interpret, reflect, challenge, evaluate and communicate the talent data that you come across. This ability to challenge the status quo, to see the data in a rational and somewhat sceptical manner to drive impartial consultative advice is critical. Often you will see other competencies mentioned within this list such as Problem Solving or Communication being subsets within Critical Thinking. There are two schools of thought/processes that are very good to keep in mind for developing critical thinking capabilities. The first technique is called the '5 Why' method. As the name would suggest, this involves asking 'why?' five times on any given problem statement to dig deep into the problem and try to uncover the root cause of the issue. The risk, though, with the 5 Whys is that you can focus very tightly and have tunnel vision; this is especially the case with complex, multi-faceted issues. This is essentially a top-down route, starting from the helicopter view and drilling down to the route.

The second thought process is a first principle theory. This is essentially a bottom-up approach, where you look at the 'lowest' or most basic truth that you know for a fact and then work up from that point to create a new novel approach that is more appropriate for your given situation.

As an example, to demonstrate the differences between these models, let's take a scenario: 'We are not able to grow as fast as we like because we cannot get enough graduates into the organization to give the talent pipeline for high performers.'

In the 5 Whys this may break down to:

- First Why – why is that?
  - o We have a large drop-off rate of graduates through the recruitment process
- Second Why – why do we see this?
  - o We see the vast majority of the graduates failing on the critical thinking part of the assessment
- Third Why – why are they failing?
  - o The candidates we are shortlisting are not strong enough in critical thinking when they come out of universities we are targeting
- Fourth Why – why do they not have this competence?
  - o The universities we have historically targeted do not have strong pedigrees in fields with strong critical thinking

- Fifth Why – why are we targeting these universities?
  - o We have always targeted these universities; it is where our founders and leadership went

If we then considered the same problem statement from a first principle perspective it could be: 'To be the company we need to be in the future, we need to have people entering the organization with strong critical thinking capabilities, as this is proven to be the number one factor for us correlating with high performance.' We then see the overall project is how to best identify critical thinking talent rather than anything related to graduate recruitment. The correct outcome could be identifying alternative universities or having no university requirements at all.

Creativity and innovation

You will often need to look for new and different solutions to problems, whether this is access to novel data sets or looking at alternative angles to find solutions. Creativity and innovation will be at the heart of this. It is worth noting that creativity and innovation are active competencies and characteristics – meaning they have to be used in a deliberate manner to achieve the desired outcome. Within our context in talent intelligence, that means ensuring you are deliberately creating the space and carving out the time to allow your team to look at creative and innovative solutions.

You also need to ensure you are giving them the security net of knowing that it is a safe space to experiment and fail. If someone tries a novel approach and it fails be sure to make them know that, as long as they had been thoughtful and learnt lessons, it is a safe space to fail. If they do not feel this, you will very quickly see them withdrawing and the creativity and innovation drying up as they will be too scared to try in case they fail. Fail fast, fail forward and always be learning.

Ability to deal with ambiguity

You will never have certainty. Your data will never be 100 per cent; you will never have the full context; the labour market will always be shifting and the business context will always be moving. Make sure you are comfortable in this zone. Plan for different scenarios and mitigate the risks, but be prepared for and comfortable acting without all the details or knowledge.

The ability to deal with ambiguity is not a competency unique to Talent Intelligence but it is one we have to flex more than most functions given the problems we are trying to solve and the data sets we are using to try to solve them. Having team members who are comfortable drilling into problems to understand which elements they need more certainty over and which elements can be more ambiguous is vital.

Think big

As I keep reiterating, this field is still new and ever changing. Do not be held back by previous preconceived ideas. Think big: be bold, be brave. This function and capability are limited only by our own creativity. Look for opportunities to challenge and stretch yourself and the team; be comfortable outside your comfort zone.

Thinking big is a competence that can both be developed and structurally driven. Look to hold 'Think Big' workshops, where you carve out time specifically to Think Big. Start with divergent thinking around a problem statement; challenge yourself and each other to be open minded and unrestricted. Do not hold back ideas: be bold, be brave and Think Big. Think about the problem from the end customer's perspective and put yourself in their seat. Do not try to go straight to the solution or be limited by current restraints; this is about ideation. Aim for quantity. Quantity was associated with quality on measures of divergent thinking customarily associated with creativity. As you develop thinking through the problem and start to look at potential solutions, start to bring in convergent thinking to solidify the ideas and offerings.

You can use this same divergent to convergent process at any time; think of it like a think big muscle that you can train and be able to turn on and off as needed.

Business/commercial acumen

This is twofold: both the ability to spot opportunities for new services and products within your customer group to develop your talent intelligence offering, and also the ability to understand how your talent intelligence work is affecting the business from a commercial perspective.

Often within HR, you see that business acumen is cited as being able to see the organization's goals, vision, strategy and to create and align activities accordingly to best serve this. For me, this leaves a large window of opportunity for Talent Intelligence to impact more broadly across the organization to really help the business achieve their desired goals.

The main reason I say this is that at present the vast majority of all of our organizations simply do not know this capability exists and yet their biggest concern is the ability to have the right people, in the right place, at the right time and at the right cost. We need to be bold; we need to be proactive and reach out and talk to these leaders. If we don't, we are doing both ourselves and them a disservice.

Data literacy

Not everyone in your team will necessarily need to be a data scientist or business analyst, but a degree of data literacy is absolutely core to all roles within your team. Whether it is data acquisition, data discovery, data cleaning, data management, data visualization or even data ethics, being very comfortable in a data led environment is key.

By its very nature, talent intelligence will have data at its core. Having team members that are strong at data storytelling, understanding when data looks out of place, understanding when to question further and dig into data sets is essential for the capability's development and further business credibility. This is not a capability that is unique to Talent Intelligence and you will see a need across your organizations to upskill the data literacy of your workforce.

Learning ability

Having a culture of learning will be key to any successful talent intelligence offering. This field is ever-evolving: the ability to learn, unlearn, relearn, absorb information readily and put this into practice effectively is vital. Unlearning is the active process of removing, or mentally parking, knowledge or skills to make way for new knowledge or skills to take their place. This ability to unlearn and relearn and the inherent curiosity it creates should run through all you do as it will lead you to constantly challenge the status quo, including your own operating models, service offerings, team alignment, etc.

One of the most interesting aspects of being able to learn and relearn is that as you do so, your brain creates new and strengthened pathways between neurons in the brain. This neuroplasticity is a physical manifestation of a growth mindset. As humans we can literally, physically choose to have a fixed mindset or a growth mindset.

These competencies should set the tone and give you the cultural context and overall framework to then be able to build each role out to specialize in their given area. It is noticeable that many of the attributes discussed above are stunningly difficult to find in most workplace environments. The cause for this is a debate for another day and another book but at its core I feel the education system in many countries is simply not designed to create individuals who question, challenge and free think around a given context or situation. The rote learning system that we see in many education philosophies relies on individuals being able to memorize and recall information efficiently through repetition. It does not look to facilitate critical or enquiry-based thinking that would be vital for any of the competencies we discussed above.

Skills and competencies for the future

In Chapter 15, we will look into the future of Talent Intelligence in more detail, but I thought at this point it would make sense to talk a little about how I see the skill set within the function developing.

In the near-term, I think we will see a continued push for high-level consulting competencies, especially critical thinking and business acumen, as we face an ever-changing labour/economic/political market. As the function grows and develops, I think we will see further specialization and compartmentalization of role type and associated skills.

I think we will see role specialization to allow pure consulting, economists, data engineering and data storytelling (as well as the all-important communications capability) to come through even stronger. Partner teams do not have the time to be our route to customers so we will see a continued presence closer to the front-line business. Being able to consult in this environment will mean increased consulting and account management abilities. These consultants will equally need to rely on specialists within the function to be the lever to pull at given times. This will see further specialization and development of data visualization, futurists, data as a service, etc. as each section of our talent intelligence product line becomes more specialized and looks to improve their own expertise and efficiency.

It is unlikely that many of these skills and competencies can be sourced within the traditional talent intelligence career path/sourcing channels (still heavily reliant on talent acquisition). I also foresee a large diversification of background happening with a large number of individuals joining the function from parallel or alternative career paths such as consulting, economics, business analytics, sales, marketing intelligence, strategic workforce planning or programme management.

Roles

Now, depending on the overall service offering you decide upon, you may have some, all or potentially none of the following roles, but this is a guide to the types of role you could think about to support the offering that you look to design. What I do not dive into here is the more sourcing intelligence or executive recruitment research type of roles around name generation, talent mapping, etc. The reason for this is twofold: first, there are many other books and individuals far deeper into the world of sourcing and executive research that have done this justice already, and secondly, I was keen to focus this section on the function that is Talent Intelligence, as I truly believe it is carving out its own niche in the corporate world.

Talent Intelligence Consultant

This is the more traditional talent intelligence consulting role that will be using data and intelligence in a consultative manner to impact business decisions. The incumbent will likely have an extensive knowledge of the talent landscape, be very comfortable forging relationships with senior leaders and their teams to enable them to use labour market intelligence to impact business decisions. They are naturally curious with a strong desire to learn and a focus on continuous improvement. They will think big, be excellent at prioritization, display strong analytical skills and earn trust quickly.

Always on Intelligence Consultant

This role is, on the face of it, very similar to both the traditional TI consultant and analyst role. One subtle, but I would argue important, difference is the nature of the work and the associated skills needed. Traditionally, both the consultant and analyst would be looking to solve specific decision points. These are single-point-of-time decisions (operational, tactical or strategic). The main difference with an AoI Consultant is that the workload itself is not one-time project based – by design, it is always on. It is a programme of work rather than a project. This means that the type of consultant can sometimes be slightly different. Once set up, the data set input, the design, the analysis and the output are all structured and in place. This role is more about understanding the changes, and the context of those changes, and being able to produce a very similar output in a repeatable and consistent manner rather than a one-off deep dive that you see in consulting.

Talent Intelligence Analyst

This role involves support with the scoping, management and delivery of talent insights and workforce projects; conducting background research and connecting to data sources wherever necessary. They will have the ability to think strategically, conduct talent acquisition focused research, act tactically on gathered research, write effectively and display strong critical thinking skills. They will usually work across all product types and customer engagement areas and will be the future talent pipeline for your Talent Intelligence Consulting team.

Talent Intelligence Futurist

The Talent Intelligence Futurist will look to the future 18 months-plus and see what headwinds you will face, what challenges you can expect, how the labour market is shifting and then recommend solutions and strategies to combat these challenges. They will systematically explore predictions and possibilities about the future of the labour market and how it will emerge from the present. It is most likely that they will have a background as an economist or a business analyst.

Communications/Knowledge Management

The communications and/or knowledge management role can often get overlooked within a Talent Intelligence team. For me, this is the single biggest error to make. Repeatedly, the biggest criticism of intelligence is that it is siloed information that does not impact as widely as it could or should due to people not knowing it exists. One solution is to install a knowledge management or content management system. These are highly valuable, and I would definitely recommend doing that, but equally they are yet one more system in the never-ending plethora of systems we are all asked to use. The effects of platform fatigue are real and getting users, and customers, comfortable on using yet another system is hard. Due to this, investing the time into standing up an effective communications strategy to push intelligence proactively in front of the relevant users is invaluable. This can be in the form of targeted newsletters, podcasts, weekly/monthly/quarterly business reviews, infographics, webinars, news alerts – whatever the mechanism your customer needs to best consume their intelligence, that is the vehicle you should choose.

Candidate Perception Research Scientist

This role involves spearheading research that leverages both qualitative and quantitative methods to understand and improve how your organization is perceived by your candidates, prospects and the market more generally. They will propose, institute and own ongoing projects to gauge the voice of our candidates across job families, geographies and businesses. Whether aligned to candidate sentiment and perception (as in this case) or a broader research scientist they will likely looking at both secondary research, as well as primary research, be it in interviews or focus groups with target populations. They will likely have a background in a social science (psychology, sociology) or quantitative discipline (maths, economics, statistics).

Data Acquisition and Engineering

The DA&E individuals will look to use a range of tools to connect to systems and extract that data for ingestion into your own environments for further processing. From performing analytical exploration and examination of data to leading the assessment, design, building and maintenance of scalable platforms, they will guide your talent clients to solve their most pressing challenges. Having an effective DA&E structure will enable your team to both scale and experiment with data in a way and at a speed you simply cannot get near without them in place.

Business/Data Analyst

The Business Analyst/Data Analyst can provide analytical support for various talent intelligence programmes and build tools to surface timely, meaningful, actionable data that will drive proactive decision-making. They will own the data and metrics needed to analyse and inform stakeholders of new and changing trends in the market. This role is often used for scaled intelligence, dashboard building, self-service tooling, etc.

Technical Programme Management

A Technical Programme Manager can be an invaluable addition to a team if you are looking at creating technical product output. They are the conduit between the customer and the technical team within your organization, translating the business requirements into a structured data need for the technical teams to build out. They will follow a similar process structure as the traditional TI Consultant since they will gather customer requirements, scope the feasibility of the project, manage the process and schedule but then given the technical, likely product and output of the project they will also rest and review the solutions proposed before finalizing the output. From a skill-set perspective they will have both a deep technical knowledge, but also very strong communications and project or programme management skills.

Product Manager

If your team is looking at developing a suite of products or moving to a self-service type model then it may be necessary to look at also having a Product Manager. This is not dissimilar to the Technical Programme Manager role but whereas the TPM is tightly engaging with the engineering team, to ensure the successful execution of the requirements gathered, the Product Managers will sit closer to the customer. They will be looking at the product roadmap, the product vision, deep diving into the user experience and pain points. Essentially, the Product Manager looks at the what (what you are building) and why (why you are building this) of the product range and the Technical Programme Manager is looking at the how (how are we feasibly going to do this?) and who (who do I need to engage with to ensure this is stable and successful?).

Data Scientist

One area that we mentioned is growing from a skills perspective and is similarly growing in a role perspective, is that of data science. Having a Data Scientist in your team can give you a real powerhouse to drive data first strategic decision-making. Data Scientists will generally have a foundation in computer science, statistics, analytics and maths and have strong analytical and quantitative skills with the ability to use data and metrics to back up assumptions, recommendations and drive actions. One thing to keep in mind though is to really benefit from a DS within your team you need access to clean, raw data rather than pre-aggregated platform data.

Summary

The skills, competencies and roles within any talent intelligence competence or Talent Intelligence function are wide and varied. The above is simply one version of Talent Intelligence; there will be more roles that evolve, more avenues to explore and more skills needed. Throughout, be mindful of what you want to achieve, what the current state is, what your own talent gap is and how you are going to lean in to buy, build or borrow the skills you need to develop the function or capability that you are looking to deliver.

TOBY'S TAKEAWAYS

- Be very clear about the skills you need across the team whether this is Strategic Consulting, Data Science, Workforce Planning or Project Management. Do not expect individuals to be able to specialize in all areas and skill sets.

- You will never have certainty. Be prepared and react in a clear and decisive manner.

- Understanding what you want to achieve with the team is vital to then be able to understand what competencies will be needed.

- This is not an exhaustive list. The skills, competencies and roles needed within a Talent Intelligence function will continue to evolve as our teams, products and industry evolve.

12

Career pathing

In this chapter, we are going to explore who, from a career perspective, comes into the talent intelligence field and what career paths are available within, through and after talent intelligence. This is a shorter chapter as a lot of the future career paths simply aren't written yet and we can explore more in Chapter 15 when we get into what the future of Talent Intelligence could be. I will not dig into the technical role specialization within this section (for example data engineering, business intelligence engineering or data science) as these roles are largely transferable across functions and the talent flows between these roles tend to be somewhat traditional and standardized. For this section, we will focus on Talent Intelligence consulting, as it is, arguably, the newer element within corporate structures and the most ill-defined.

Inflow

Let us address the low-hanging fruit early on. The majority of inhouse Talent Intelligence teams are created from within Talent Acquisition functions. Given this, it is understandable to expect that a lot of the talent coming into talent intelligence comes from Talent Acquisition roles and this is certainly true. The majority of inhouse teams created in the last three years have had their Talent Intelligence team members and especially leadership come across from sourcing and talent acquisition. There are the odd exceptions, with some phenomenal individuals coming in through the knowledge management and librarian path, coming in parallel from executive assistants or chiefs of staff or coming across from competitive intelligence. However, as a rule, these internal Talent Intelligence teams that are housed in TA are being staffed by TA individuals and, as we saw in Chapter 11, even if they want to pivot, given the skills they would like to reduce within the function, they currently have their core deliverable outputs still very tightly aligned to TA and Sourcing.

This talent acquisition career path is true for internal Talent Intelligence functions, but when we look at the industry more broadly we see a very different trend. When we take a broader view, we see the majority of Talent Intelligence professionals coming either from other intelligence industries (marketing intelligence, competitor intelligence, etc.) and transitioning to talent intelligence early on before developing up or coming in as graduates and being developed from scratch. This is particularly apparent in the vendor/platform and outsourcing industries where we see a very strong onboarding, development and career pathing of talent intelligence professionals.

What does this mean? One thought that comes to mind for me with this is that we are almost limiting our experience and exposure by design by converting so many talent acquisition professionals over into talent intelligence roles. We are limiting our diversity of background, diversity of thought and diversity of exposure. This will likely limit our thinking and our abilities to develop as a function. Many internal Talent Intelligence functions are trying to avoid this in a few ways:

- Many are starting to exploit the vendor landscape by co-locating their Talent Intelligence functions in the hot spots for talent that these vendors create (such as in Bengaluru*) and looking to bring in their experience in scaling talent intelligence operations that we simply have not had at the same scale internally historically.

- I am seeing a growing trend to bring in individuals from alternative career paths, such as intelligence, economists, psychologists and in parallel to this, seeing growing appetite for intern and rotation programmes to both develop the team's capacities and capabilities but also challenge their traditional thinking.

BENGALURU

*At present we see a large percentage of the world's Talent Intelligence professionals sitting in Bengaluru, India. This is largely due to both CEB Talent Neuron and Draup having a large footprint there, both originally being created by Zinnov. This has created a talent intelligence ecosystem with 'client' teams looking to co-locate in Bengaluru to match this. At the time of writing, Philips,

Atlassian, JP Morgan Chase, EY, Wipro, Intel, Accenture, Infosys, Google, GSK, Information Services Group and Qualcomm among others, all have individuals in Bengaluru with a talent intelligence skill set; many of them coming from the Zinnov-created firms.

Outflow

Currently, lack of career progression is the number one reason people are leaving the talent intelligence field. They simply cannot see enough development routes ahead of them. The skills within Talent Intelligence consulting are highly transferable and we are seeing individuals move through the field into several areas, such as back into Talent Acquisition, into broader People Analytics, Talent Management, strategic consulting, Economic Development, Market or Competitive Intelligence, Compensation and Benefits, Human Resources, Strategic Workforce Planning or Programme Management, to name a few.

Having said this, we still see most talent intelligence individuals moving roles within the field once they enter, moving from one Talent Intelligence role to a similar role at a new company offering new opportunities or moving from a mature team to a newly created team to set up their offering. This is still a new field and the opportunities are plentiful.

This movement, though, is largely a product of teams not growing and developing at the same rate as the individuals within it. As we will discuss in the next section, one route to help give clarity is to develop a Career Pathing Roadmap (CPR) for your Talent Intelligence function.

Career pathing roadmap (CPR)

The CPR is an excellent career framework tool to give clear and transparent guidelines to your team and managers around role responsibilities, levelling expectations, salary guidelines, promotion requirements, etc. that should both explore the individual contributor and the manager pathways. You should be able to clearly articulate how functional dimensions change by level, whether that is dealing with ambiguity, the scope and influence of the role, the customer base, the levelling of execution versus advisory, the ability to impact change or the level of process improvement responsibility but also the suggested experience for each given level.

So what could this look like? Let us work through a couple of roles/levels to see what this could look like:

Business level: Corporate Grade 1.

Individual contributor/manager: Individual contributor.

Title: Talent Intelligence Analyst.

What you do: You are a single-threaded owner responsible for the planning, execution and delivery of straightforward projects related to an existing programme or account.

Degree of ambiguity: Works on defined projects. Will occasionally need guidance.

Scope and influence: Generally, works with one team to influence their project plans, stakeholder and customer interaction.

Business development: No business development responsibilities; work is provided.

Advises: Peers, consultants.

Execution: Defines requirements, facilitates progress, identifies blockers and increases the visibility of issues.

Impact: Moderate. Team goals and project-related metrics.

Process improvement: Improves team efficiency. Optimizes previously defined processes.

Suggested experience: Relevant direct or transferable experience in analytics or intelligence fields.

You will be considered for promotion to Corporate Grade 2 if you consistently demonstrate a combination of the following:

- You work independently to successfully manage difficult, cross-functional projects.
- You are proficient at transforming raw thoughts into clear, consistent, accurate documentation and/or direction.
- You keep the scope of effort under control and accelerate progress, or operational efficiencies by driving crisp and timely decisions, identifying and clearing blockers, and escalating appropriately.
- You improve team processes and metrics; you unblock delivery and reduce costs.

Then the next role could be:

Business level: Corporate Grade 2.

Individual contributor/manager: Individual contributor.

Title: Talent Intelligence Associate.

What you do: You are responsible for managing an existing programme or account, delivering difficult projects aligned with team goals.

Degree of ambiguity: Internal strategy is defined. Business problem and solution may not be defined. Delivers independently but will seek direction.

Scope and influence: Generally, works across teams. Influences their customers' internal roadmap priorities and decisions. May influence external entity interactions. Begins to mentor.

Business development: Minimal business development responsibilities; work is largely provided.

Advises: Consultants, Managers.

Execution: Work is tactical. You will manage difficult and/or cross-functional projects/goals. You are able to spot risks and ask the right questions. Clears blockers and escalates appropriately. Comfortable making trade-offs: time versus quality versus resources.

Impact: Moderate. Multiple team goals and program-related metrics. May impact a country or region.

Process improvement: Improves project and process efficiency. Optimizes cross-team processes that improve team efficacy and delivery.

Suggested experience: Relevant direct or transferable experience in analytics or intelligence fields, building account ownership and owning multiple team goals.

You could then break out into far more detail around what behaviours and expectations are at these levels, such as leadership examples, mentoring or developing others, educating the broader customer base, etc.

This structure should be followed right through the entire CPR up to and including the leader of the team. You should have clear visibility of how to join as an entry-level individual and see the entire career path available within the team including all levels, responsibilities and expectations. It is important within this to offer a Y-shaped career path where career progression is not limited only to management but rather you have multiple paths available, one with management (Team Leader, Junior Manager,

Senior Manager, Executive Manager, etc.), but also a path for individual contributors to progress and develop without having to take on management responsibilities (Consultant, Senior Consultant/Engagement Manager, Principal Consultant, etc.).

Summary

There is currently an imbalance in the talent intelligence field with more roles than individuals but equally not enough large and structured teams to allow for sustained career development and career pathing. We are seeing individuals move roles or move out of the field altogether to try to further their own self development. To address this, we as an industry need to offer both more development and growth as team sizes grow but also we need to get more explicit about the career paths and development routes available. We need to ensure that as an industry we are bringing in diversity of background across all areas to look to maximize opportunities moving forward. We also need to ensure we are creating robust and clear career paths and that individuals have a clear line of sight as to how to grow and develop their careers.

TOBY'S TAKEAWAYS

- Create clear, Y-shaped career paths showing development or role, scale and scope to enable your team to see their careers ahead.

- We are still as inhouse teams largely reliant on Talent Acquisition teams as a main source of talent for our Talent Intelligence functions. Look to challenge the status quo and build diversity into your talent pipeline.

- The skills learnt in Talent Intelligence are highly transferable and in demand. Use this as both a selling point of the function and be aware of the risk this exposes you to from a career pathing and talent outflow perspective.

13

Inhouse and partner landscape

Building a Talent Intelligence capability can feel daunting but you should not feel alone. In this chapter, we are going to explore what teams are available both internally and also look to the broader partner landscape to work and co-create with.

Internal partners

There will be a plethora of teams that can help and support any talent intelligence development and capability or functional build-out. The following is a dive into a few of these but please do not see this as an exhaustive list. The beauty of this field is that there is so much scope for experimentation and development. Go and explore functions not mentioned here and see what room there is for collaboration and co-creation. This field will only be limited by our imaginations.

HR Analytics (HRA)

As discussed previously, with caveats, HRA can be a very natural fit for any Talent Intelligence function to be housed or set up but even if not the home team they can be a fantastic partner and internal resource.

By their nature HRA have a natural directional context for your Talent Intelligence work. They will have an understanding of your subject matter and understand some of the challenges you face. Quite often HRA will have access to the back-end analysis for the internal tooling, giving you an instant partner for your projects. They also have the technical skills needed to report on, analyse and hopefully forecast out on this data, giving you an excellent capability that is often currently missing in Talent Intelligence functions (as discussed in Chapter 11).

There is also the subject of their output. Talent intelligence will help give context to a lot of the key metrics that HRA are reporting against, analysing and forecasting out on an ongoing basis for the business. This external contextual data will be invaluable in making their analysis more holistic and robust. Not only can they be a great partner team but also a customer team.

Finally, there is the element of data governance and data maturity. By its nature, talent intelligence is a new field and is still finding its feet. Partnering with more mature functions that are used to dealing with such sensitive data sets can really enable teams to develop and challenge their thinking around data governance. What is our data strategy? Who is responsible for any data gathered and where is this stored? How is the data processed and analysed? Where is this associated analysis stored? Who uses the data, where and why? They can really help ensure you are setting your TI offerings up on a solid data foundation.

Real Estate

One of the most powerful partner teams to align with is Real Estate. Real Estate will often know the grand location vision and strategy. They will be engaged in at senior levels within your organization and have an eye to both the current pain in capacity management and planning and an eye to the future of where the organization wants to move. This could be looking at:

- different locations (high cost to low-cost country for example)
- moving from a central office culture to a hub-and-spoke model with main corporate hubs and satellite offices offset as spokes
- highly remote environments or a hybrid

Whatever the future of work and future of the workforce vision that you see ahead, it will be Real Estate that have to bring this vision to life operationally.

RE also will have fantastically granular data on the cost of physically entering a new location. This helps to ground any Talent Intelligence analysis, as it is one more element in building the full picture. For example, moving to a new city for cost savings could absolutely make sense for your core talent intelligence study from a workforce cost perspective but if the real estate is five times the price then it may not make sense overall. Equally, you may make recommendations for a fully remote workforce but if RE can see that the infrastructure just is not in place to be able to enable that at scale in a stable way, then it may not make sense organizationally.

The sort of questions you can look to answer in partnership with Real Estate could be:

- What locations are we looking to depreciate/launch/expand in the next five years?
- What does our manufacturing footprint look like in ten years' time?
- What does our footprint look like in a hybrid work environment?

But then, once again, once overlaid with Talent Intelligence input:

- What locations are we looking to launch/expand in the next five years and how feasible is that given the market/competitor landscape?
- What does our manufacturing footprint look like in ten years' time and how will that change given automation and changes in the workforce?
- What does our footprint look like in a hybrid work environment and how will that land with target candidate profiles?

Finance

Finance is a partner team that often fall between the cracks for Talent Intelligence teams but can both be hugely powerful and a very valuable ally.

First and foremost, within the talent context, Finance will set the direction and budget ahead. This means that any strategic workforce plan or labour market feasibility will need to align with that budget and plan to stand a chance of success. Although, as we know, workforce planning should be an always on programmatic campaign, always looking to the future to see movements and headwinds, in reality these activities are usually project based and tied around the annual budget planning cycle. Finance will often set this budget in a top-down model by looking at aligning budgets to corporate goals before then reversing this to a bottom-up model for headcount needs capture for individual teams or business units. As discussed in Chapter 5, this is a fantastic point to inject talent intelligence to set feasibility of location/headcount numbers, etc. but more importantly this allows talent intelligence to align at a very direct and strategic level in a mechanism that the business leadership both value and understand. This can be invaluable in setting the tone as being holistic labour market trusted advisers.

Also, it is worth remembering that Finance will have all this data stored centrally, so as you work through the year on location strategy, organizational design strategy, etc. it is very valuable to once again tie back with Finance to see how your talent intelligence advice sits and aligns with the strategy from a finance perspective.

Finally, Finance can be fantastic partners to work with to articulate the measurable business impact of any given problem statement. So instead of, 'Location X is seeing an increase in attrition by 5 per cent', you may be able to work with Finance and look at the workforce productivity loss or potential customer penalties for missed targets. The problem statement then becomes: 'Location X is seeing an increase in attrition by 5 per cent, both meaning we are seeing a $5 million loss in terms of productivity and leaving us exposed to $30 million in potential customer penalties for missed targets.' This helps ground the talent intelligence work in measurable impact and business measures that leadership can understand.

Compensation and Benefits (C&B)

A function that talent intelligence can often run the risk of challenging and being challenged by is Compensation and Benefits/Rewards; but this need not be the case. C&B is a subfunction of HR that is specifically focused on employee compensation, recognition, rewards and benefits. This will cover both the direct compensation (employee pay and bonus) and broader benefits (long-term incentives/share offerings, bonus schemes, parental leave, health cover, etc.).

On the face of it, C&B and talent intelligence should make for natural partners but often you will see the challenges between the two worlds due to compensation data seen within talent intelligence and the data sets C&B will use for their work.

Broadly speaking, talent intelligence teams will look for as close to real-time compensation data points to reflect any market movements and changes in competitor compensation that may affect their immediate talent risk exposure (be it in attraction, acquisition or attrition). To do this, most talent intelligence teams will use vendor data where they have it available but also couple this with publicly reported and publicly available data. This could be self-reported data by individuals in feedback forums, self-reported data in surveys, published data on job boards, published data on competitor websites, published data from H1B applications, etc. This is in stark contrast to most C&B teams, who will often buy in macro salary benchmarking reports from large data benchmarking companies. This data is reported by companies and is highly validated. C&B teams will use this in conjunction with reviewing internal data (such as the number of offers going out of range or the number of candidates leaving for compensation reasons) and align them with their overall compensation philosophy (such as upper quartile, mid quartile, heavily reliant on base salary, heavily weighted towards bonus or stock units and so on) to then set the tone for the given period ahead.

This means that often there is a conflict between the internal C&B philosophy and what talent intelligence teams (and recruitment teams) will see and feel in the marketplace. This can lead to a potential conflict situation.

I would recommend aligning with C&B as early as possible to align these different perspectives. Use the rapid changing external lens to help C&B:

- design a compensation philosophy that will be attractive in the market, be it salary or overall package
- benchmark your offering against competitors
- be the voice of the market around changing candidate trends (benefits needed for remote work versus on site, changes in appetite for stock units versus base salary, etc.)

This is not a one-way street though. Look to use their data to help align and set parameters to ensure your recommendations are aligned with the overall corporate philosophy. Also, look to use their expertise to guide on C&B recommendations and set subject matter expertise context for data you are seeing in the market, etc.

Marketing Intelligence (MI)

As we discussed back in Chapter 5 when we were discussing Always on Intelligence (AoI), your Marketing Intelligence function can be a hugely interesting partner team and internal resource. Not only are the skill sets very complementary, but also the output, customer base, commercial mindset and even research tracking and knowledge management tooling all align with talent intelligence very closely.

The research tracking and knowledge management tooling cannot be overlooked. These are fundamental elements to have in place to enable you to scale. The project/research tracking is absolutely key to know what workload you have on, what is in the pipeline and how this work is aligned to your customer groups, metrics, goals, KPIs and those of your customer. It is certainly possible to buy the appropriate tooling from an external vendor, but often you will need to see first what is already available internally. Work with your other intelligence-based teams to see what they already have in place and see where you can align. More often than not, they will be facing similar challenges and you can look at things holistically from the start, rather than looking to potentially combine or merge later down the line.

In the past I have 'repurposed' both candidate CRM systems or collaborative project management systems to look at having clear project tracking across the team. As long as you can store, track and run management information out of the tool (so you can scale), be open minded about the tool selection.

On the knowledge management front, see what is already in place with MI. If you are in luck, they will have a content management or knowledge management system already in place and they will allow you to 'plug in and play' from a talent intelligence stance. If not, look at the process they are doing around research storage and sharing and see if there are opportunities to co-create or look to improve the offering.

Talent Acquisition

As we discussed in Chapter 7, Talent Acquisition (TA) can make for a natural home for Talent Intelligence but, as we will find out, they can also be a fantastic partner team and resource. All the way back in Chapter 2, we looked into HUMINT (Human Intelligence), as intelligence generated through conversations with employees and candidates can be huge – and hugely under-utilized – sources of information. Looking to partner with your Talent Acquisition colleagues to curate this intelligence is the secret weapon for many Talent Intelligence teams.

TA spend all day, every day, talking to candidates from competitors. They will know what is going on across all levels of the organization: redundancies, growth areas, salary changes, performance review structures, bonus pay-out periods, skill-set changes, leadership challenges, role or remit, scale or scope. They will have handles on all of this information among other things. The hardest part is to build a mechanism to capture this intelligence, aggregate and tell the story of the intel. This mechanism should be built into standardized processes (such as CRM/ATS fields at telephone interview stage) as much as possible to ensure intelligence is a by-product of natural TA activities.

Do not despair though; you do not have to build these mechanisms immediately. Look for the low-hanging fruit and easy wins – simply talk to TA. When you are looking into specific locations, talk to the recruiters who work that market; if you are diving into specific job families, talk to the recruiters who handle that job family and ask about the challenges they face. What do they see as roadblocks to recruitment? What does the competition look like? What would they like to see voiced/changed by leadership to make things more successful? It is simply amazing how much rich intelligence you can gather simply by talking to recruiters and getting a voice of the market.

As well as being a great source for scaled intelligence and a fantastic resource for route to customer (as discussed previously), TA is also a wonderfully complementary partner team when it comes to looking at any kind of rotation programme into Talent Intelligence.

All of these are merely the tip of the iceberg. Look to explore your functions to see where there is room for cross-fertilization of ideas; this could be Talent Management, Sales, Product Design, Organizational Design and so on. Every function will have elements of expertise that you can work with, learn from or partner with. Go and explore.

Partner landscape

One resource that can and should be investigated for support is that of your existing vendor and partner landscape. Once again, the following should not be seen as an exhaustive list but rather a starting point to help you think about the types of relationships that may be in place and how you can look to work with them from a Talent Intelligence perspective.

Recruitment process outsourcing (RPO)

Many of the larger RPO organizations are starting to scale their Talent Intelligence capabilities. If you already have an RPO in place for your recruitment needs, this can be a clear and clean path for building a talent intelligence capability for your organization. If your RPO of choice does not have this muscle developed yet, all is not lost. RPOs by their nature will see a large swathe of the market and have an incredible insight to the candidate perception, salary benchmarking, market positioning, etc. Look to really partner with your RPO and (as you would with your internal Talent

Acquisition team) look to build mechanisms to capture their insight on a regular and ongoing basis.

We are also seeing a movement with some of the larger RPO firms looking to take advantage of the large data sets they gather through their business activities to launch their own talent intelligence products and benchmarking tooling. This is an interesting development and is complementary to the more traditional Talent Intelligence vendor. The former can offer closer to real-time reflections of the candidate market, channel optimization, the ability to drive primary research into hyper targeted talent pipelines, etc. and the latter often takes the more macro view, combining government and global level labour and economic data and combining this with data from social footprints. The two can be combined to give a fascinating view.

Recruitment advertising

Look to have active conversations with your recruitment advertising partners. They will have a wealth of information about not only your own campaigns and success rates but also, similarly to the RPO, real-time reflections of the candidate market, channel optimization, the ability to drive primary research into hyper targeted talent pipelines, etc. No other source will have as broad a view of the active candidate landscape than some of the large recruitment advertising job board organizations. They will see elements unique to their offering such as, but not limited to:

- Talent relocations. How many software developers based in city X are looking at jobs in city Y, for example? This is also interesting as it is an early predictive indicator rather than a reactive piece once someone has already moved.

- Candidate desires. What is the talent market looking for in a job? The most recent mass example is how many candidates are searching for 'remote jobs' or 'hybrid working' but this could equally relate to job titles, skills and specific company brands.

- Candidate behaviours and persona. What is their preferred medium to apply on (mobile versus computer)? What time of day do they want to apply? How long do they spend reading a job advert? Essentially this looks to consider what the candidate persona is.

This data is all-powerful in itself but becomes incredibly powerful once overlaid with other data sets such as brand perception, candidate perception, channel conversion metrics, competitor intelligence, location data, etc.

Recruitment agencies

Recruitment agencies have a unique space in our talent intelligence eco-system. They often will have a wealth of information on your employer brand, candidate perception, candidate desires, salary benchmarking, competitor movements, competitor growth, etc.

It can be a more sensitive partnership to leverage due to their broader customer base possibly being your competitors and many won't have a commercial model in place to necessarily build a talent intelligence partner-ship more formally but if they are a trusted partner I would certainly recommend talking to them about exploring what support and co-creation opportunities could be available.

Marketing/recruitment marketing partner agencies

If your organization has a recruitment marketing or employer brand team, it is likely that they will have a whole partner and vendor landscape for you to explore. Some of this information may fall into core Marketing Analytics but there is a lot of useful information around brand perception (especially when overlaid against candidate perception), channel optimization or conversion metrics, broader social economic or diversity data, etc.

Benchmarking organizations

There will be organizations that your company will likely already partner with for various benchmarking data points. This could be broad Human Resources benchmarking data around organization design, specific func-tional benchmarking data such as Talent Acquisition benchmarking organ-izations, right through to compensation and benefits benchmarking data. You will likely find challenges in place and restrictive usage for much of the benchmarking data but it is worth exploring this for two main reasons. First, if you can gain access such benchmarking data can be invaluable and a huge resource to leverage. Secondly, it shows your internal points of contact that you want to align and look to work in similar spaces. This can be a fantastic way of having open initial conversations before aligning goals and strategies.

Talent Intelligence vendors

As we look at the external partner landscape, the final partner we will look at is your core Talent Intelligence vendor. The vendors in this space are an absolutely crucial and critical partner to you as you look to establish a talent intelligence muscle or Talent Intelligence function. Look at your needs, talk to potential vendors and be clear about your needs and business case. They can help you frame the data and ensure success. They will work with a full range of Talent Intelligence teams, seeing the full spectrum of offerings, and will be invaluable in terms of understanding what 'good' looks like at any given stage. Don't see them purely as a service or data provider: they are some of the strongest talent intelligence capabilities in the industry with some of the most creative and innovative talent intelligence minds. Really build the trust, build the relationship and look to build together.

We are incredibly blessed in this industry that we have a vendor landscape that is hungry to develop, partner and co-create to help internal functions grow, mature and thrive. They are incredibly busy in the community, which can be in groups such as the Talent Intelligence Collective, running podcasts, writing white papers on best practice, offering guidelines on tech adoption, maturity models for Talent Intelligence, offering data or support to those in need or simply being active in the group discussions and evolution.

This includes Stratigens supporting the Talent Intelligence Collective Podcast and providing the support to enable it to happen every month or collaborating to run the world's first-ever Talent Intelligence Awards in 2021. Mercer, EMSI, Horsefly Analytics, Armstrong Craven and Talent Intuition came together in 2019 with Marlieke Pols from, at the time, Philips to write one of the first, if not the first, white paper on Talent Intelligence – 'Talent Intelligence Why, What and How: A guide to commercially successful Talent Intelligence in a digital era'. Numerous vendors offer their support daily in the Talent Intelligence Collective groups both on Facebook and WhatsApp with different reports that they have pulled together to show insights on the market. Indeed Hiring Lab, with the awesome team of Pawel Adrjan and Jack Kennedy (among others – the full team is here https://www.hiringlab.org/about/), produce some of the most insightful labour market insights and are open to presenting these for free at events to help to educate the industry about the challenges ahead. We are truly blessed.

Summary

There are lots of resources and partners, both internally and externally, that will have shared goals and aligned vision to what you are looking to drive in your talent intelligence offering. Look to map these and actively look to partner and co-create with them. This will ensure that you have a more robust data, product and intelligence offering but also a more comprehensive approach to your labour market intelligence.

TOBY'S TAKEAWAYS

- Find your internal teams to partner with by initially looking at your mutually-aligned goals and aligned data sets.

- Be open minded with data sources and partner teams to listen to their goals, processes and strategy; more often than not, you will find a point of mutual interest or benefit.

- Don't be afraid to talk to your vendor landscape; they will likely want to co-create and experiment. They may not realize the value of the data they have at their fingertips to you as the end customer.

- Be thankful for the awesome Talent Intelligence vendor landscape. They truly are helping shape the future of this industry.

14

Examples of use of talent intelligence

Company case study 1

A global defence organization identifies new target industries for talent acquisition

Stratigens™ increased the talent pool of a global defence sector organization by 88 per cent by identifying new target industries for talent acquisition. This data was used to prove they had access to the skills supply needed to deliver government contracts. The data supports all government contract bids.

THE CLIENT
One of the top 10 players in the world in aerospace, defence and security, with revenues of more than €10 billion.

THE CLIENT PROBLEM
The business had a clear view of their internal talent pool, a good talent management strategy, a great early careers programme, good leadership development and good visibility of the gaps in their talent pool. But an ageing workforce and long-term contracts meant that the client had real gaps in their senior engineering talent pool to fulfil existing contracts. The balance between their early careers talent and their experienced talent would soon tip the wrong way. As a result, they urgently needed to understand the pool of available talent and identify whether there was an obvious place to put a regional engineering hub so they could attract and retain this experienced talent in a highly competitive market. The business needed to prove skills supply to win contracts.

THE SOLUTION

We identified the total pool for senior engineering talent (10–15 years' experience) in the UK, split by specific skills type, including chemical engineers and structural engineers.

HOW WE HELPED

A total of 39 specific skills were identified and analysed across the total engineering pool in the UK. To complement this, our data science team was able to identify previous and current industries, previous and current companies and the universities from which this talent had graduated.

THE OUTCOME

Data from Stratigens surfaced that 41 per cent of the overall talent pool for this business was within a commutable distance of existing locations. Therefore, the business did not need to establish a new regional hub. This decision saved the business millions of euros in set-up costs. Stratigens skills-based analysis found that 88 per cent of the talent pool for this organization is outside the defence sector. Based on their current model, the business was only accessing 5 per cent of the total talent pool. Stratigens data opened up a talent pool of thousands – expanding the organization's talent horizons. Analysis from Stratigens identified new target industries for talent acquisition for this business. The data on future talent supply has been used in the bid process to inform government contract bids. An in-depth understanding of talent supply and demand has helped this organization to win major new contracts by proving continuity of skills supply.

Company case study 2

Informing the location strategy of a global engineering business

Stratigens data enabled a 5000-plus headcount tech engineering business to compare locations for software engineers. Our data informed the firm's real estate strategy, ensuring they were in the right places to tap into rare skills.

THE CLIENT

A leading tech engineering business with offices in the UK, US and Australia and more than 5000 employees.

THE CLIENT PROBLEM

Having grown through acquisition, this business had a number of different office locations globally, with software teams dispersed around many of the locations. There was a plan to grow the team considerably and the CHRO wanted to understand where in the US they should do this to optimize availability of talent and cost. The client had two of their existing locations in mind and needed to understand the talent market for software engineers in each so they could inform a real estate decision.

THE SOLUTION

Using Stratigens, the client was able to search across both locations, looking for software engineering talent that was within a commutable distance of each office to see key data on the talent market, including supply and demand, plus other factors that contribute to a location decision. Stratigens surfaces data on skills availability, competition for skills and which organizations you would be competing against for the same skills. Plus, it offers other location-related data such as cost of living, transport, infrastructure and the ease of doing business in a place. This information is combined to make a recommendation on the best location. Our client could see how many software engineers there were in each location, the proportion of the market that was dispersed across industries and the live demand for software engineers in each region. Additionally, they could see what current salaries were being advertised by others in order to attract this talent.

THE OUTCOME

Stratigens data showed that from the firm's current list of offices, competition for software engineering talent was significantly lower in location X compared to other locations. This information informed the company's strategy, saving them recruitment costs and ensuring they were in the right place to attract the talent they needed. More importantly, they were able to see how small the market was and to feed this data into their strategic thinking to determine how to maximize both markets.

Company case study 3

Helping a global FMCG company to find digital marketing talent pools

Stratigens helped a global FMCG with 80,000 employees identify new sources of talent to transition the business from operating in a B2B environment to B2C. Data on four cities including talent supply and demand, business risk and commercial property cost enabled them to make an informed entry into the market.

THE CLIENT

A global FMCG made up of approximately 50 brands, with more than 80,000 employees in more than 55 countries, that serves the nutrition and health needs of pets every day.

THE CLIENT PROBLEM

This global FMCG business was used to operating in a business-to-business environment and had been hugely successful with this model for many years. Technology changes, a more globalized market, a changing consumer profile, and a different approach to consumer buying are all disruptive forces affecting this business, with change happening at pace.

As a result, the business needed to start interacting directly with consumers. This was a change that meant the businesses needed to attract hire and retain talent with profiles that they had never needed before. Just one of the new skills they needed was digital marketing. As a traditional FMCG, our client's existing sites are manufacturing-based and in locations suited to this environment.

The HR and Strategy Director knew this was not going to be the right approach to be competitive in this new talent market. They wanted to understand the talent markets in four locations globally: San Francisco, Hong Kong, Paris and London. The client wanted to understand the supply and demand for talent, the impact of entering each market, the talent attractors for digital marketing and the talent model they should adopt.

THE SOLUTION

Using Stratigens, our client was able to see how many digital marketeers there were in each location, the industries that hire the talent and the live demand in each city, including the demand for permanent versus freelance roles. Additionally, they could see what current salaries were being advertised by others in order to attract this talent. As importantly, they were able to draw key data on the HR environment, business risk and ease of doing business in each city and the cost of commercial property. They were able to bring together talent data with key financial metrics to understand the cost of locating a team in each city and the risk associated with each along with key financial metrics.

THE OUTCOME

For the first time, our client could make a decision quickly with HR, talent and financial data all in one place. As a direct result, they were able to clearly differentiate between the four locations based on the supply-to-demand ratio for digital marketers. Typically, this type of project would take between 21 and 30 days for a research team to complete. Stratigens gave them answers in seconds, so they could make an informed entry into the market in order to be a step ahead in their talent acquisition and to take a proactive approach to managing the disruptive forces on their business.

Company case study 4

Informing the employer brand of a global defence business.

> Stratigens informed the employer branding strategy of a global defence business that wanted to extend its reach for senior talent beyond direct competitors. Stratigens identified sources of talent with lean manufacturing experience outside traditional talent pools.

THE CLIENT

A market-leading defence business that offers state-of-the art solutions to protection and security for a number of leading defence and space businesses and national governments.

THE CLIENT PROBLEM

A new Group Operations Director from a different industry wanted to understand the senior operations talent within a commutable distance of their site in the South West. Historically, the operations teams had come from defence backgrounds and directly from competitors. Our client realized that the business was a high-volume, low-margin operations environment. The business needed best in class, lean manufacturing experience.

THE SOLUTION

Using Stratigens, we were able to run a high-level search illustrating the numbers of senior operations individuals within a commutable distance of the site. Additionally, we were able to see the demand for this talent to understand how competitive the marketplace was and the salaries that were being offered to people with this level of experience. Importantly, we were also able to identify the industries employing this talent now.

THE OUTCOME

The business was equipped with a data-driven view of how competitive the marketplace was, and they knew what they needed to do in order to compete for best-in-class talent. More importantly, the Group Operations Director was able to demonstrate that the talent required was in a number of different industries and that by restricting their talent attraction to the defence and space industry, the business was severely restricting the talent pool and experience of talent available to the business.

Company case study 5

How we averted the costs of poor location planning for a global engineering consultancy

> Stratigens averted the costs of poor location for a global engineering consultancy by providing insight into early career talent. By analysing 1300 data sources and 1.5 million profiles in under an hour, Stratigens helped the company save millions in real estate investment.

THE CLIENT

Our client is a global consultancy, with more than 3000 consultants operating across a variety of industries.

THE CLIENT PROBLEM

This consultancy was producing a report for their client on engineering talent in the UK. The end client wanted to understand where to locate a regional hub for engineering in the UK. They needed to understand the size of the market, the hot spot locations for engineers and the universities that the talent had come from. Their challenge was that this data is in thousands of different sources, in an unstructured format, and it would be time consuming and cost prohibitive to produce the report for their client.

THE SOLUTION

Using Stratigens, we were able to produce a report that showed the hot spots regionally, the levels of experience and the early careers pools for engineering talent. We were able to produce this data in less than an hour using Stratigens to scan more than 1300 different data sources and more than 1.5 million UK engineering profiles. Stratigens produces widgets of insights in a highly visual way that the consultancy was able to lift and import into their report.

THE OUTCOME

The consultancy was able to produce a report for their end-user client within a one-week period at a cost that was acceptable to both parties and not prohibitive. As a direct result of the data derived from Stratigens, they were confidently able to say that there was not one regional hot spot location for engineering talent that could serve the majority of their client's needs. As a result, they saved their client millions of pounds in building a new location and were instead able to make recommendations on where to site the talent based on their existing locations, based on a different approach to internal talent management.

Company case study 6

Using Talent Intelligence to inform the diversity strategy of a multinational energy company

THE CLIENT

The client is a global energy company with a commitment to low carbon and a net zero ambition. Meeting this ambition requires wholesale business transformation including skills transformation, a major part of which involves building a more diverse workforce.

THE CLIENT PROBLEM

Like many organizations, our client faces challenges in meeting its goals for diversity, which feed into the organization's cultural and inclusivity objectives. Diversity is priority for the CEO and, as one strand of activity, our client wanted to benchmark their organizational composition against the external talent market.

Understanding the diversity of their internal and external availability (at a skills level) would help the client identify where they should focus their efforts in order to achieve greater diversity across the business.

Our client wanted to provide recommendations to the board to set diversity ambitions for the future that were data-led.

THE SOLUTION

Our client used proprietary data and analysis from Stratigens to analyse the diversity of external skills populations in the US, UK and Europe against a range of critical job families. The Stratigens team extracted and mapped skills and diversity data to client specific workday skills and job families based on the client's internal systems. This data was mapped to the client's grades, levels and leadership populations accordingly. The dataset extracted and analysed included more than 350 million profiles.

Grade mapping in the external market included combining not only experience and skills, but also company size to ensure that the data was all relevant to our client's context. To ensure the project remained on track, the Stratigens data team held weekly meetings with the client's internal data team.

THE OUTCOME

To support the client's inclusive hiring strategy, the internal data analytics team used Stratigens data to generate a dashboard for the CEO, business leaders and talent acquisition teams. The dashboard clearly showed the client's internal headcount by grade, job family and location alongside gender and ethnicity, against the available external population (also by grade, job family and location). The dashboard also showed candidates by applicant stage and hiring manager screen – both broken down by gender and ethnicity.

Using Stratigens data on an ongoing basis, this data will be refreshed every six months to provide the senior team with a current lens on diversity. This data will be used in conjunction with the client's internal talent data to enable scenario modelling. The internal data analytics team will be able to model the company's diversity ambition from 2022 to 2030 based on matching the market through hiring inclusively.

Company case study 7

A broadcast and utilities infrastructure company understands the talent landscape for rare and niche skills

> Stratigens analysed the skills landscape for rare and niche capabilities for our client. This work identified major new talent populations for the business and at least 20 channels through which to source talent. The business now has a clear line of sight to future talent and has identified internal reskilling opportunities.

THE CLIENT PROBLEM

This leading UK broadcast and utilities infrastructure company faced a challenge in hiring sufficient engineers to meet the needs of their growing and evolving business. Where talent supply is scarce, hiring managers frequently resort to hiring expensive contractors to bridge the gap.

The Chief People Officer wanted to understand the talent landscape for engineers within the UK to help meet their talent supply needs. The client wanted to explore the composition, location and employment preferences of experienced engineers to enable them to identify the skills gap. The client also wanted to get a fresh lens on future talent planning using talent intelligence to inform skills development.

THE SOLUTION

Using Stratigens, we identified the potential talent pools for engineers by six specific skill sets. We provided a comprehensive picture of talent supply by UK region, along with intelligence on the largest industry and company employers, for these skills.

We then identified future sources of talent by exploring the original sources of talent including education, location and first post-education role to build an understanding of early career paths. We also reported on the companies with which our client is competing for this talent.

We found variations in supply and demand between the six specific niche skill sets, with some being extremely rare. In some cases, we found fewer than 10 individuals with the specific blend of skills that the business needs.

Although the talent landscape is fragmented and without one dominant employer of these skills, we found that 48 per cent of the company's in-demand skills are in one specific industry but that there is also a potentially large untapped talent pool originating from a different career background.

> The facts generated from Stratigens challenged some long-held beliefs and opened our eyes to options that had previously been discounted or not even considered. Small changes to the way and where we advertise roles has significantly improved candidate quality and that data has given confidence as to where we invest and specifically decisions around what we buy versus build. The data has enabled a different conversation between the People function and business leaders, building trust and engagement in the process and approach to hiring and developing talent within the business.
>
> Chief People Officer

THE OUTCOME

Data from Stratigens is being used to inform the business on how best to mitigate resource capability gaps. Because there is a better understanding of talent supply and demand across the UK, the HR team can identify potential external talent sources and also direct internal development towards the specialist capabilities that will need to be developed through upskilling.

Intelligence on the presence of a second wave of target skills in similar and related industries has enabled the business to tap into new potential sources of talent. Our analysis, which included educational backgrounds and generational split, has reconfirmed the use of modern apprentices as a longer-term strategy in nurturing specific skills.

Our client is seeking to hire relatively scarce, hard-to-find skills. Individuals with these skills are active across more than 20 social channels, including some lesser known and niche platforms. The insight provided by Stratigens includes recommendations on how, and where, the talent acquisition team can seek to cast their net.

Company case study 8

Raising the game of talent intelligence at a global med-tech firm

> Through the provision of strategic labour market data, including via Stratigens, the TI function is supporting the senior leadership team in making informed decisions about skills supply and locations for its growing business.

THE CLIENT PROBLEM

The Talent Intelligence function is a small team in a 40,000-person organization and so, in order to conduct research, technology platforms play a big role. Our client has been using Stratigens as one of its data sources to help make major business decisions, such as how to access niche skills and where to locate its global service centres.

One of the challenges that our client was tasked with when the function was established was to encourage the senior leadership team to look at talent data and to get them to start thinking about talent, and the data behind it, differently. The relationship that the senior team has with Talent Intelligence has already evolved significantly since the creation of the function.

Whereas in the past, the leadership team might look to the TI team to validate decisions already made, the business now looks for talent intelligence information at the beginning of the journey. One of the goals as the business moves forward is to get data more deeply engrained in day-to-day decision-making.

> Data is becoming the norm and talent intelligence is out in front, not just confirming decisions that have already been made. In the early days I had a location analysis question, but the decision was made before our research was finished. The business chose the location that would have been third or fourth on my list. Fast forward to 2021 and we're operating very differently, working with Stratigens to proactively guide on location strategy.

THE SOLUTION

Using Stratigens, the TI function produces regular reports that inform long-term talent strategy. These labour market reports include an analysis of seven key job families, providing an overview of key roles within job families, data on talent supply and demand, high-level cost and high-level diversity metrics.

The reports offer guidance on where to focus and include data on hot topics, for example, remote working and connectivity. They provide the basis for conversations about future planning, not just one year out, but looking at a long-term time horizon from a talent perspective.

These reports are released at the end of the first quarter of the financial year so that the senior leadership team and working groups can review the data in order to plan for budgetary discussions that take place at the end of quarter two.

> As a data-person I think it's really important to be able to look at data and compare to see where there are trends. When the data comes together, I get a really strong picture that I can combine into a report. The senior team appreciate that talent intelligence has something that we can bring to the table that they don't have.
>
> Manager of Global Talent Intelligence

THE OUTCOME

The reports produced for our client have raised the game of talent intelligence and increasingly the senior leadership team are asking for deeper dives into data. The conversations that the TI function has with leadership demonstrate that there is hunger for talent intelligence data and value within it.

The Talent Intelligence function collaborates with other teams at a senior level, including HR, people analytics and talent acquisition, to present a joined-up picture with an external lens. The next step is to help leadership and talent teams to look at day-to-day talent trends that are happening now and that can impact talent decisions, for example by looking at competitive talent intelligence.

In the future, the manager of global talent intelligence would like to see a move towards more dash-boarding and self-service so that colleagues can see and manipulate live talent intelligence data. Plus, once the business has a base of data to look back historically as well as forwards, they'll be able to be more predictive about spotting future trends.

Talent intelligence is ensuring that at this med-tech firm, no talent decisions are made in a vacuum and that all have a strong basis in data. Although a small team, the Talent Intelligence function is providing an invaluable picture to the senior leadership team through an external talent lens.

> We chose Stratigens as it provides a unique outlook on the jobs and skills in the global workforce. I was impressed with the holistic view of skills and location analysis. Using Stratigens, we are able to access quality, targeted data to help us make strategic talent decisions today and tomorrow. For example, we're using the platform for site location analysis, to identify the best locations to find specific in-need talent, and to provide competitive and market intelligence.

> Manager of Global Talent Intelligence

15

What does 'good' look like?

When I started this book and thought about the chapter titles, I wanted to include a chapter to really set out a benchmark of what 'good' looks like for us as an industry and as an output. However, throughout researching for and writing this book, I have concluded that there is no 'good'. As discussed in Chapter 8, I do believe there is a maturity model that we can aim towards but fundamentally 'good' for you and your company at this given point of time will be very different from 'good' for anyone else, or in fact for you and your company in the next six or twelve months and into the future.

One thought that came to me throughout this time, and as a reflection of running my own Talent Intelligence teams, is that of a 'good' product output. With all the teams that I have created, I look to have what I refer to as 'bespokeable standardization' of my teams' output. No matter who in the team does a report, no matter what region, what customer group, what business area and so on, the report should look and feel the same. Absolutely I want the report to be customized to the customers' needs, but the brand of the team should remain the same; the standard of work should remain high and the quality of the product should remain high. Any leader should be able to pick up our work and instantly recognize it as a piece of our output.

This led me to think about Talent Intelligence teams, our output, 'good' and how successful this 'bespokeable standardization' approach has been. Overall, I am happy with the approach and think it has certainly enabled teams to land better but one thing stands out to me. Talent Intelligence consulting is much like cooking, and consultants much like a chef. Let me expand: if you took 10 chefs and gave them the same ingredients, and asked them to produce the same output/recipe, you will end up with 10 different meals. All will be very similar, and all would have followed a similar preparation, methodology and cooking process, but you would still end up with very different results. This is due to the given experience levels of the chefs, their own culinary career path, their own flair and ability to bring the best out of the ingredients. I feel that this is very similar to what I see from the top-performing Talent Intelligence consultants. They can take the same raw materials/data but by using their own experiences, their own flair and ability to cut, dive into and analyse the data in unique and interesting ways, they are able to pull together very different, yet familiar offerings.

Certainly, you can lock down the ingredients list; you can lock down the recipe and the cooking process and make it a step-by-step guide, forcing the chefs to conform and produce a far more consistent product but with each output not necessarily being quite as strong as any individual chef could produce. Similarly, you can do the same in talent intelligence. You can lock down the data sets, lock down the project inputs, create step-by-step guides for a given type of project and produce a very consistent output but that creativity, curiosity and flair will be lost. I would strongly suggest you keep that creativity, curiosity and flair.

Now, although I do not want to be explicit about what 'good' means, what I can say is that to scale a Talent Intelligence team you need to root your work in impact. Look to your organization and the problems you are facing. Look at the pain points and really look to tie your work to the most critical and impactful work. If you cannot position the work in this way, look to work with those partner teams, especially finance, to see how you can reframe your existing work to demonstrate the impact most effectively. Be clear about what you are as a function (Chapter 6): what are your vision, mission and goals? Is your work enabling you to achieve that? If your goal is to be informative then simply delivering the talent intelligence in a fast and efficient manner is success and 'good'. If you are looking to solve problems, then look back on work completed and ask if this problem has truly been solved; if so, then congratulations you have achieved 'good'. If you are wanting to create a function that makes recommendations to senior leaders, look at what you have completed and how many recommendations were made and/or adopted; that will give you your benchmark for 'good'.

Benchmark case studies from companies

So, although good is very subjective, it is very valid and useful to have some kind of benchmark – a line in the sand, a north star or a point of reference

– to know how you are developing and how you stand compared to the industry. With this in mind, I thought it relevant to look into some organizations that are doing Talent Intelligence and see how they are structured, their offerings and their 'good'. This is by no means exhaustive but should make for some interesting comparisons and in the spirit of Talent Intelligence this section was compiled using OSINT methods, looking at readily available and publicly available information unless a contributor is named. As with any OSINT activity, it should be taken as directional, with all the pitfalls of publicly available data, and I would always recommend cross-validating with primary sources where possible.

Amazon Web Services (AWS)

Amazon Web Services is a subsidiary of Amazon that provides on-demand cloud computing platforms. AWS Global Talent Intelligence (GTI) is focused on driving data-driven acquisition strategies for tech and non-tech roles globally across AWS. They run regional talent intelligence programmes and global projects/programmes that drive efficiency into the top of the recruitment funnel. The team supports multiple business lines/functional areas within AWS and provides strategic guidance on market research, competitive intelligence and talent mapping efforts.

They will also partner with Employer Brand, Learning and Development, Diversity, Workforce Strategy and other HR Teams to influence AWS location strategy, diversity talent acquisition strategy and build versus buy talent programmes.

Amazon Web Services Talent Acquisition's Global Talent Intelligence's mission is to accelerate the process of finding candidates of all backgrounds using research, insights and programme management tools to enable Amazon Web Services Talent Acquisition's teams to reach their strategic goals. AWS GTI also aims at enabling AWS business partners to make informed talent decisions.

The AWS GTI Global Program aims to be a force multiplier for AWS TA by empowering recruiters and sourcers with research and talent intelligence, to create efficient talent strategies for today and cultivate talent pools to support AWS' growth tomorrow.

This section was created using publicly available information from a job posting for a Head, Global Talent Intelligence, AWS Workforce Planning Research & Science, various job adverts for Business Intelligence Engineers, Senior Talent Intelligence Lead and Strategic Program Manager.

ADP

Automatic Data Processing (ADP) is an American provider of human resources management software and services with 58,000 employees and $14.59 billion in revenue. The HR Innovation and Analytics team within ADP is responsible for transforming Human Resources with science, technology and human intelligence. They work to increase data-driven insights to assist their leaders in making better people decisions in an effort to add value through improved business outcomes or a better associate experience.

ADP were recently (at the time of publishing) looking for a Talent Intelligence Lead to join them to look to leverage external labour market data, internal data and research to inform talent and recruiting strategies. They foresaw that the role would partner directly with executives and hiring leaders across the organization to inform and educate them on talent trends and market data that will positively influence business decisions globally.

From the responsibilities listed within the role, we can see that some of the core activities of the team were broad but with a real focus on creating a commercially-minded function with competitive intelligence at its core. They are tasked with conducting talent intelligence, market research and analysis for various roles and business areas across multiple regions. They see this role as a strategic function that provides input and thought leadership on talent trends and the future of work. Competitive intelligence around the core HCM and technology space came through as a key area of responsibility and to really be the voice of competitive talent intelligence within the HR function. Similarly, they were tasked to really dig into the competitor landscape to understand best-in-class competitors, emerging niche players, strategic threats and future opportunities related to the ability to attract, develop and retain talent. Once again, we see a thread on competitor knowledge flowing through with a desire to give Talent Acquisition and hiring leaders a competitive edge by creating battlecards to allow them to compete in the talent market across various geographies and role types.

This section was created using publicly available information from a job posting.

Philips

Philips is a Dutch health tech organization, with 80,000 employees and a €17.2 billion turnover, founded in 1891 in Eindhoven in the Netherlands.

In 2016, the Talent Acquisition team at Philips could see that there was an increased ask from their business stakeholders to look at competitors, skills and labour market data in a much more commercially-minded way. As an organization, they were pivoting from a consumer manufacturing organization to a health tech group but their real estate footprint, their Employee Value Proposition, their skills and their business was not designed for this fundamental change. Business leaders, and in turn HR leaders, looked to their Talent Acquisition team to help provide the data, insights and intelligence needed to drive this change, with the formation of a Talent Intelligence function in June 2016.

Philips looked to approach this in three key ways.

- First, to affect the decision-making process and control their talent demand internally and not just be positioned to go after the external supply side. This was done in two main ways: an increase in talent intelligence consulting to effect decision-making across the organization and the creation of a workforce modelling tool to enable scaled self-service access to relevant decision makers.

- Secondly, it was vital to increase the competitiveness of their talent offering and to give recruiters the insights they needed from both Philips and their talent competitors to go into career conversations that positioned Philips and their Employee Value Proposition aggressively in the marketplace. This was done by launching a programme that created a number of competitor High Value Target (HVT) battlecards (as discussed in Chapter 5) to enable recruiters to have insights at their fingertips at all times to be able to attract key skills from targeted competitors.

- Finally, they took a far deeper look at target candidate populations and created personas around these populations bringing a far deeper level of recruitment marketing analytics and insights into the fold.

These steps led to some very impactful outcomes across Philips. This included, in 2019 alone, delivering savings to the business of €10.5 million through effective right shoring of business operations. In no small part due to the battlecard programme, 26 per cent of all hires in software engineering for Philips came from those companies highlighted and targeted as HVTs. Finally, the internal Talent Intelligence consulting team had an estimated financial impact of €953 million with €3 million in cost avoidance from external research firms.

Kimberly-Clark

Kimberly-Clark (K-C) is a FMCG organization with 46,000 people and $19 billion turnover (2021), including brands such as Huggies, Kleenex and Andrex.

K-C's Talent Intelligence department looks to collect and analyse market data on the regional labour markets, competitors and business practices, using this information to give them a competitive edge in securing the top talent in the marketplace. They then look to use this information to influence business decisions and strategy as well as steering, regional and local Talent Acquisition attraction strategies.

Typical offerings include looking at location feasibility, the labour market, pay scale, quality of installed talent, volatility, etc. They try to select competitor high-value target companies through market research while conducting gap analysis to understand how K-C fares against competitors. They look at talent movements and highlight any key people movements or company updates across the given market, business or function. They also look at more macro labour market trends, hiring scarcity, talent flows and any kind of mergers, acquisitions and lay-offs or re-organizations that talent competitors may be going through.

This section was created using publicly available information from a job posting for a Regional Talent Intelligence Lead and information from their corporate website.

Microsoft

Microsoft's Global Talent Acquisition organization's mission is to engage and hire the people who empower the planet. They play a vital role in delivering on the promise of Microsoft's culture and, ultimately, make a difference in the world through how and who they recruit. Their Talent Intelligence function is the team responsible for delivering excellence in who and how they recruit at Microsoft. The GTI function is seen by their Talent Acquisition organization as the authoritative source for research and analysis of the external talent landscape, partnering across the business whether by business unit, region, function or market to develop global, cross-company talent strategies focused on solving for critical talent needs, maximizing emerging opportunities and responding to evolutions in the talent market.

Enabling Microsoft's talent strategy is absolutely key to this team. One of the main elements for the team is to look at the organization's multi-year strategies and hiring goals and use internal cross-business data, and external labour market data, to provide insights and trending information to help guide these strategies and goals. Competitive intelligence is also key, specifically when tied to the competition for talent and how it can be used to build talent pipelines. They also work closely across the organization to look at the company's talent strategies focused on critical technical or leadership talent gaps.

This section was created using publicly available information from a job posting for their Director, Talent Intelligence.

Meta

Meta, formerly known as Facebook, is an 80,000-person, $118 billion-revenue technology powerhouse.

The Global Talent Intelligence (GTI) team at Meta is tightly aligned to their aggressive talent growth strategy. A main goal of the function is to design strategies for the recruiting organization to find and hire the world's greatest builders and achieve diversity goals.

The team looks to build a scaled approach to unlock strategic differentiation and recruiting team effectiveness. The team is laser focused on using data and labour market research to challenge business problems to support the right hiring outcomes for Global Recruiting, which is their core customer. They are very conscious though that recruitment does not sit in isolation and look to work with much broader stakeholders including People Analytics to ensure alignment on priorities and initiatives across the organization.

The team's typical types of activities could include talent pool analyses, location assessment, competitor landscape or diversity insights.

This section was created using publicly available information from job postings for an APAC Talent Intelligence Analyst and a Business Analyst and Meta's corporate website.

Google

Google is a tech giant with 140,000 employees and a turnover of $256.7 billion. Google's talent intelligence team is called Talent Intelligence & Insights team, often referred to as Ti2. This team sits as part of the broader People Operations function, who go by the motto that they 'find them, grow them and keep them'. Across the function, whether recruitment, development or broader HR, Google look to have a data-driven approach across the board.

Google is a company of builders and problem solvers and their Ti2 team is no exception. They expect individuals to use analytics, market research and intelligence to solve complex challenges and to create and provide predictive insights to help clients make the best talent decisions.

Talent Planning is at the core of Ti2 and they look to engage with stakeholders to design and implement highly effective, results-driven research strategies for global talent planning initiatives and intelligence projects.

Google see that the power of talent intelligence needs to be broader than just recruiting or HR and they see a core part of their role to develop consultative partnerships with both recruiting leads and HR partners but also wider Google executives and other business leaders to maintain a pulse of business and recruiting activities.

This section was created using publicly available information from a job posting for a Global Talent Consultant, Talent Intelligence and Insights based in Singapore.

SAP

This section has been completed with insights and input from Teresa Wykes, Global Head, Talent Intelligence at SAP.

SAP is a German technology giant with more than 100,000 employees and a €28 billion turnover that focuses on enterprise software to manage business operations and customer relationships.

The SAP Global Talent Intelligence team is a new strategic pillar under the Global Talent Attraction organization. The main responsibilities of the team are proactive talent engagement and attraction strategy and providing market intelligence and talent insights. The purpose of this is to enable SAP to continuously be a leader in hiring the best talent and to support the business in making workforce decisions.

The team looks to guide senior business leaders and senior HR leaders to make smarter workforce decisions by using talent insights and really building the trusted adviser relationship. They are also keen to ensure they remain close to the business and local outcomes. One of the key areas for this is that the team look to own the market unit/country candidate generation responsibility by developing and deploying strategic talent attraction initiatives that align with regional directives, for all levels of talent except early talent. This includes building, engaging and nurturing the talent pipelines across the identified skill segments to ensure a 'ready-now' pool when a hiring demand arises. Talent Intelligence at SAP also owns external succession management and regularly showcases and arranges socialization of this talent with the board. This is a multi-channel and multi-faceted approach to engagement using both online and offline mechanisms such as LinkedIn, their CRM and other sources such as Meetups, networking, conferences, etc.

The other key area is market intelligence; analysing competitor activity across a number of talent variables to help create content and propositions that position SAP favourably with the talent they seek to hire, as well as educate the business.

This section was enriched using publicly available information from a job posting for a Talent Intelligence Engagement Consultant, SAP iXp Intern – Talent Intelligence Consultant, Talent Intelligence Consultant for EMEA and a Senior Talent Intelligence Consultant.

Stryker

Stryker is a 46,000-person, $17 billion-turnover medical technology company based in the United States.

The Talent Intelligence team within Stryker sits under the TA Innovation Senior Manager. The key role of the Stryker Talent Intelligence team is to deliver talent market research that informs talent strategies across Stryker. The TI team has two core pillars: Labor Market Research & Competitive Intelligence and Talent Analytics Capability & Development.

Within Labor Market Research & Competitive Intelligence, the TI team would look to collaborate with HR, Talent Attraction and the core Talent Acquisition teams to look to inform and craft a talent strategy that is driven by data analytics and insights. They would own global talent mapping of total talent supply and demand in order to assess Stryker's competitive position and pinpoint high-value sources of talent, be it across key functions or market regions. From a communications perspective they will be required to research industry trends, market information, including talent migration, competitor intelligence and share interesting findings with stakeholders across Talent Acquisition and the business in monthly/quarterly/annual labour market insights.

On the Talent Analytics Capability & Development side of the function, they are looking to build scalable self-service solutions that align to reporting and analytics strategies across HR using both internal and external data sets.

This section was created using publicly available information from a job posting for a Talent Intelligence Associate Manager.

Salience Data

This section has been completed by and with thanks to Barry Hurd, Chief Digital Officer, co-founder at Salience Data.

WHEN AND WHY WAS YOUR TEAM FORMED?

Our focus on understanding the fundamentals of growing and maintaining competitive talent ecosystems was based on the fact that our team had launched multiple talent products, solved for organizational problems with hundreds of hiring organizations over our careers, and knew that building the best product meant having the best team. Our organization was formed in 2016 as a response to trends in digital innovation to create new business models and high-growth team structures. The various start-up and corporate ecosystems were locked in a cycle of hiring the wrong people for the wrong phases of each initiative and were burning through endless amounts of investment capital. The concept of creating a supporting innovation team was often rooted in technology, product development, research and data. As strategic viable models were constructed, there was an increasing need to understand and deploy talent intelligence, covering a wide range of corporate ecosystems and support levels, ranging from internal expertise mapping, vendor capabilities and talent acquisition

WHAT IS YOUR TEAM'S MISSION/VISION?

The Matrix provides the next step of innovation with a lot of choices. Some of them look like Judgement Day, while others imagine us living in a corporate world of mega cities living under the rule of robotics. We believe there are really smart people playing different sides and not all of them are good. So we made a team of folks who believed in doing good things for good people. We encourage our clients to make the right decisions for the right reasons. We build teams of innovators who want to create something better for everyone, not just the few.

WHAT ARE YOUR KEY PRODUCTS/SERVICES?

We address complex market issues in innovation, digital transformation, model development and market trends for industry leaders. Our talent-oriented services include a range of market research, employee network analysis, industry development strategies, team development, modelling development and investment justification.

WHO WOULD YOU DEFINE AS YOUR KEY CUSTOMERS?
Corporate teams in high growth with an innovation overlay; start-up/VC incubators/accelerators. They have an inherent need to leverage data across talent, market and industry trends to launch a new product or pivot laggard services into new revenue lines.

ARE THERE ANY SUCCESS STORIES YOU WOULD LIKE TO HIGHLIGHT?
Unlike many firms, we don't take credit for our clients' work. We don't claim how our strategies shifted billion-dollar funnels or what crisis we helped them avoid. We get our work by being networked with some of the best and brightest minds across dozens of categories and know how to be team players.

HOW DO YOU THINK YOUR TEAM WILL EVOLVE IN THE NEXT FEW YEARS?
We'll continue to hire and train our network. We've spun off a few teams that have launched public-facing services and help us grow our network of understanding.

Qualcomm

This section has been completed by and with thanks to Arnab Mandal, Strategic Workforce Planning Lead at Qualcomm.

WHEN AND WHY WAS YOUR TEAM FORMED?
Qualcomm look to leverage both internal employee data and also external labour market data around geographic trends, talent intelligence and competitive insights to help inform a more holistic people strategy. I was hired to lead the Workforce Planning and Talent Intelligence team to cater to business challenges from a talent perspective.

WHAT IS YOUR TEAM'S MISSION/VISION?
Qualcomm's Strategic Workforce Planning team is an HR Centre of Expertise that focuses on providing workforce planning, competitive intelligence and talent analytics capabilities to help our executive leaders plan

their future state workforce design and roadmap. The mission is to help provide a holistic view of the internal and external talent landscape, so we can ensure we have the right skills, in the right locations, at the right cost and at the right time.

WHAT ARE YOUR KEY PRODUCTS/SERVICES?

Our core offerings are talent insight studies, battlecards, newsletters, job posting analysis, internal headcount and compensation tracking and forecasting, attrition studies, etc.

We systematically and periodically provide the business updates on competitor job postings and analyse skill clusters to identify potential sources of talent, such as start-ups and university research teams, for our future hiring needs.

Our data teams partner with several workforce planning vendors to provide insight on talent pool availability at various locations. They also look at potential employers, university pipeline, diversity, cost, infrastructure and other factors to provide insight on established and emerging talent hot spots.

WHO WOULD YOU DEFINE AS YOUR KEY CUSTOMERS?

Our key customers are Engineering/Business, HR Business Partners, Talent Acquisition and Diversity & Inclusion.

HOW DO YOU THINK YOUR TEAM WILL EVOLVE IN THE NEXT FEW YEARS?

We want to develop detailed headcount forecasting models which will help the business and finance have better control over talent spend.

This section was also enriched using externally publicly available data.

BP

This section has been completed by and with thanks to Daorbhla Smyth, Talent Intelligence Manager.

BP plc is a 60,000-person British oil and gas company headquartered in the UK with a $164.2 billion turnover. They have a bold ambition to be a net zero company by 2050 or sooner and help the world get to net zero. In order to do this, attracting, employing and retaining the right talent will be absolutely vital.

WHEN AND WHY WAS YOUR TEAM FORMED?

We were formed in January 2021. Following the company's transition from an international oil company to an integrated energy company, there was a need for Talent Acquisition to understand the external market better to inform key strategic talent decisions required to make the company successful and competitive.

WHAT IS YOUR TEAM'S MISSION/VISION?

Everything that we do is in service of an even better experience, for our people, customers and candidates. We drive this through quality, timely insights and strategic partnerships.

WHAT ARE YOUR KEY PRODUCTS/SERVICES?

External skills analysis, competitor talent analysis and market mapping

Talent Intelligence within BP is multifaceted but this line of sight back to the ability to hire and attract the right talent is at its core. The talent intelligence team will work closely with talent sourcing and market intelligence to plan and implement global sourcing strategies. Looking at the market and creating creative and inventive sourcing solutions are core parts of this function. The function has two main elements: Market Insights/Intelligence and Sourcing Intelligence.

Some of the key activities they perform in Market Insights include advising the business on the most effective strategy for their recruitment goals in any given geography or talent pool. They are also seen as the voice of the market on industry trends on new technology, talent sourcing techniques and using these insights to improve the existing strategy.

When we look at their Sourcing Intelligence pillar, we see some of the core activities being around Talent Acquisition Analytics, looking at core channel and funnel conversion rates of the recruitment funnel. We also see that sourcing strategy is absolutely vital given data-led thought leadership and advisory and ensuring the sourcing strategy is in line with their candidate experience and diversity and inclusion commitments. We also see some more traditional sourcing activities in that they will look to directly source candidates for strategic sourcing and continuously expand the company's pool of potential candidates.

The key customers for the BP Talent Intelligence team are business SVPs and VPs, and talent integrators.

Through competitor and skills insights, BP's Gas & Low Carbon Energy business were able to define a talent development strategy that will support the broader expansion of BP's hydrogen business in line with the commercial scale-up of the organization. This activity also led to the identification and successful hiring of our VP Green Hydrogen Solutions. As the industry talent intelligence analysis was developed internally, rather than seeking consultancy support, the team created a cost saving of circa £120,000.

HOW DO YOU THINK YOUR TEAM WILL EVOLVE IN THE NEXT FEW YEARS?

Closer partnership with internal people analytics teams to create more holistic insights and early interventions, helping BP remain competitive in the market. Also, building on synergies with executive search and strategic workforce planning to support the identification of top talent and develop a focus on nurturing this talent for the future.

This section was enriched using publicly available information from a job posting for a Talent Intelligence Lead Advisor.

TOA Global

This section has been completed by and with thanks to Jose Mari Garcia, Head of Talent Intelligence, TOA Global.

WHEN AND WHY WAS YOUR TEAM FORMED?

We were originally formed in March 2022. We were formed as an upgrade from the Talent Sourcing Team that assists in recruitment operations for our BPO firm. Since our previous Talent Sourcing Team focused on administrative processes in recruitment, we were upgraded to the TI team to focus on the following: headhunting, recruitment marketing and data reporting.

WHAT IS YOUR TEAM'S MISSION/VISION?

To be a world-class talent team that delivers quality candidate experience and business growth.

WHAT ARE YOUR KEY PRODUCTS / SERVICES?

As a company, our services are offshoring accounting and bookkeeping services from the Philippines to clients in Australia, New Zealand, Canada, UK and the United States.

As a team we look to plan and implement creative, cost-effective and data-driven talent sourcing strategies. We identify, manage and evaluate proactive talent intelligence plans, position-specific sourcing strategies, initiatives and tactics including networking, internet job boards, database mining, referrals, advert response, professional outreach and advanced sourcing techniques. We determine and implement appropriate lead generation techniques for market industry, skill sets, profiles and regions.

WHO WOULD YOU DEFINE AS YOUR KEY CUSTOMERS?
As a company, businesses in Australia, New Zealand, Canada, UK and the United States.

ARE THERE ANY SUCCESS STORIES YOU WOULD LIKE TO HIGHLIGHT?
We are giving jobs to 200 Philippine accountants and bookkeepers every month. We give local accountants training and international certification to be globally competitive. We partner with communities, academe and organizations to level up careers for people.

HOW DO YOU THINK YOUR TEAM WILL EVOLVE IN THE NEXT FEW YEARS?
As a fully-staffed team with heads and members of: strategic sourcing, recruitment marketing, candidate care, data management, research and analysis.

This section was also enriched using externally publicly available data.

Shopify

This section has been completed by and with thanks to Jennifer De Maria Senior Talent Market Researcher at Shopify.

Shopify is a Canadian-based multinational e-commerce company, headquartered in Ottawa, Ontario, with more than 10,000 employees and a turnover of $3 billion.

WHEN AND WHY WAS YOUR TEAM FORMED?
Formed in 2020, initially to direct sourcers to a more targeted approach in finding talent. Requests evolved into finding diversity data, benchmarking programs and procedures with other industries and competitors to more complex, nuanced requests.

WHAT IS YOUR TEAM'S MISSION/VISION?
To combine internal and external data, while aligning with the business, to give directional insights on challenges.

WHAT ARE YOUR KEY PRODUCTS/SERVICES?
Labour market digests, reports and analysis, answering problem statements.

ARE THERE ANY SUCCESS STORIES YOU WOULD LIKE TO HIGHLIGHT?
More people know what TI is and acknowledgement from senior leaders on breadth of data insights has helped amplify the discipline.

HOW DO YOU THINK YOUR TEAM WILL EVOLVE IN THE NEXT FEW YEARS?
More headcount and recognition of the impact TI can have in an organization.

Summary

We can see that 'good' is entirely subjective and you are only in competition with yourself to continually push and challenge this benchmark. Do not rest. If you are satisfied with 'good' and the world around you is moving forward, changing and adapting, then there is a high likelihood that your definition of 'good' is no longer relevant.

TOBY'S TAKEAWAYS

- Look to create 'Bespokeable Standardization' as a framework to allow your Talent Intelligence chefs to be able to flex their creativity and flair.
- Do not overly concern yourself with 'good' within other organizations. Absolutely look to benchmark your work and look to develop your own offering but remember that good is entirely subjective.
- Keep developing. 'Good' will always be moving, pushing forward towards the horizon. You need to ensure you are ruthlessly chasing it.

16

What is the future of Talent Intelligence?

This is an exciting time for Talent Intelligence – with no roads well-trodden ahead and options available to us as both an industry and a function.

The Talent Intelligence technology industry's future

As we discussed way back in Chapter 1, we are currently in the second main wave of products and platforms within the talent intelligence field. Most noticeably in this wave, we have seen a large influx of talent intelligence platforms that address more talent management and internal analytics at their core versus the more traditional externally focused talent intelligence products.

Expansion

We are currently in a period of unprecedented investment into the HR tech ecosystem. The Covid 19 pandemic and associated labour shortage meant firms spent more on their HR tech than ever before to try to understand their workforce and the labour market better. Couple this perfect storm of high demand, low supply, high attrition and spiking wages along with a venture capital industry with money burning a hole in their pockets and you end up with a situation where investment is at a level never before seen. Through this we are seeing new platforms launching ever more frequently, each with their own angle on the data, the product, the customer focus, etc.

But how will this play out in the longer term looking to the future? I see a few main themes coming through.

Acquisition

Even though the total number of platforms is growing dramatically, we are already seeing the first shoots of a consolidation of platforms with EMSI and Burning Glass coming together. I think, as I look to the future, there will be a natural selection process that will occur with many platforms merging or being taken over. This may be from a market share perspective, to enhance product offerings or gain new market entry, but there are simply too many vendors given the overall customer base for this to be scalable and sustainable. Equally, I foresee that as the market tightens and we see a recession rolling down the road, many of the firms that have the investment capital will feel an added pressure to provide a return on that investment in a harder market and will look to exit sooner than initially planned.

This could especially be interesting when you look at the opportunities that present themselves when you combine the internally-focused talent intelligence vendors and the externally-focused talent intelligence vendors. Imagine: an ATS with real-time external labour market feasibility data for the hiring manager as they're creating a requisition; or a performance management system that could highlight the talent flows of your top performers; or a compensation system that is directly plugged into the market to also show what candidates are demanding and competitors are paying... or an attrition monitoring system that tracks leavers and highlights flight risks in their old team given the leaver's new company and the new roles created.

There are so many options available with the range of talent platforms on offer and the synergies between them.

Specialization

One alternative route ahead I see is hyper specialization of product. This is something we have seen in many broader software vendors in more mature markets, especially post-market reckoning and acquisitions/mergers, where smaller vendors could not compete at the scale of the larger vendors so decided to hyper specialize to carve out a market niche. This may well be a secondary market change that we see evolving.

But what could that look like?

It could be a Talent Intelligence platform that is designed around the nuances of a specific industry. How does talent intelligence for mining differ from technology, retail or oil and gas?

Equally, it could be targeted around a tightly defined customer base. What would a talent intelligence platform designed specifically for venture capital firms look like and how would that be different from a multi-industry enterprise org or a small FMCG firm?

It could be to cut via role or skills. How would a platform heavily invested and customized for software engineering intelligence be different from one designed for sales, finance or marketing intelligence?

Platform ecosystem

Another route I see developing in the future is a pure platform play where vendors act as a data lake or a hub platform. More and more I see customers looking for data access beyond the traditional vendors' platform view. They are needing API access and the raw data to be able to cross-fertilize and combine with their own internal data sets. I think one evolution of this from a vendor perspective is to become a data as a service/ecosystem vendor, where they not only offer the data access to the end customer but also open this up for other vendors to be able to create their own custom offerings on top of the data sets. The best example of a platform ecosystem that comes to mind when I think of this evolution is the game platform called Roblox (apologies – I have kids and they like to game!). Roblox is an online gaming platform with around 64 million users. As well as creating their own games, Roblox allows users to create and play games created by other users, as well as purchasing specific in game 'add-ons' that can enhance the gameplay but also provide a revenue stream for the creators (not necessarily Roblox).

What could that look like in a Talent Intelligence ecosystem? Imagine a Talent Intelligence vendor that not only creates their own talent intelligence suite of products but also allows their infrastructure and data set to be used by users, customers, other vendors, academics or be open platform for anyone to experiment and create new solutions. This platform ecosystem evolution will allow for specialization, custom integrations and experimentation in a way well beyond the current vendor offering as the barrier to entry for new vendors, the massive data lakes needed and associated costs, would be so much lower.

The Talent Intelligence function's future

As we discussed in Chapter 7, there are a number of functions where Talent Intelligence can find a home; some more natural than others. When I look to the future, there are two paths that seem most interesting to me. Let us explore them both now.

Centralized Intelligence

This is an interesting concept of having one centralized intelligence centre of excellence that runs across all disciplines across the whole organization. This would see functions such as Talent Intelligence, Competitor Intelligence, Market Intelligence, Marketing Intelligence and Business Intelligence come together into one Centralized Intelligence CoE. At first this may seem a tad 'left field', given we have just spent an entire book detailing the intricacies of Talent Intelligence and how more often than not it is a very separate, albeit complementary, offering of other functions and offerings including other intelligence teams.

However, there are a number of things that a Centralized Intelligence CoE could offer that could be very interesting to explore. The model I would foresee is my ever-favoured centralized but ringfenced model, i.e. a Centralized Intelligence CoE but ringfenced by:

- product offerings: being Talent Intelligence, Marketing Intelligence, etc.
- business units: with each BU having a tiger team of TI, MI, BI, etc. all working independently for that BU
- market: as with the BU but cut by market, with each market having their own fully holistic (TI, MI, BI, etc.) and self-sufficient Intelligence Unit

Skills

From a skills perspective, although, as previously discussed, there are some fundamental differences between the various intelligence pillars, there are equally some opportunities to centralize and align skill sets for growth and economies of scale. There are several skills, whether hard or soft, that absolutely flow between the various pillars of data literacy, data visualization, data storytelling, commercial acumen, stakeholder management and consulting skills, which are all very fluid and transferable.

This centralized CoE would also afford the luxury of allowing individuals to flow between offerings, allowing them to both develop their skills across the areas and also reduce skills bottle necks and de-risk the function.

Offerings

One of the most interesting aspects of this model is the ability to look at both exploring adopting products that other intelligence teams offer, such as Talent Intelligence adopting Always on Intelligence from Marketing Intelligence, but also exploring where the offerings are complementary and you could pull in various elements to create a combined intelligence offering. This gives leaders and decision makers a far more complete picture than they have ever seen to date.

War gaming is an excellent example of where we can see some of this combined thinking coming together. A war game is a workshop/exercise where you role play a scenario by putting yourself in the position of your key competitor. How will they react to a given situation? What levers will they pull to react? How will they countermove our strategy? You then look to step back into your own shoes to see how you could counter these positions. If you were looking at running war gaming workshops, how much faster and more interesting would they be if run from a holistic Centralized Intelligence CoE rather than from separate teams being pulled together?

Knowledge management

One of the biggest challenges of any intelligence group is that of knowledge management, communications and duplicative work. Centralizing everyone into one team and one community, having centralized systems, processes, tooling and a knowledge management platform means that you can greatly reduce this duplicative work and increase knowledge transfer across the organization.

Intelligent systems

Much of what we have discussed above is looking at existing systems, processes, tools, teams and looking to align them more effectively for each other and for the end customer. One area though that is really interesting when we look to the future is that of intelligent systems and within a Centralized Intelligence CoE this would really come into its own. Intelligent systems would be systems that are looking to use machine learning, artificial intelligence, predictive analytics, Robotic Process Automation, etc. to allow your intelligence organizations to make faster, higher quality, more repeatable and more impactful decisions and recommendations. We can take predictive analytics as an example. Using this in isolation for Talent Intelligence, looking to predict competitor courses of action is arguably possible but the data sets, data cleanliness and direct correlation are all in their infancy. If we looked to combine this with Marketing Intelligence that can also see the competitor's product direction, market penetration rates and investment areas, we can suddenly look to unlock far more interesting prediction models with greatly increased forecast accuracy.

This model also moves out of our 'customer' base into a centralized control mechanism. At first this feels counter-intuitive, but this allows intelligence teams to truly be data and intelligence led rather than trying to find data and intelligence to confirm a predetermined outcome as can happen if you are embedded in a business line or function. This view is seeing our core offering being intelligence and centralizing around that concept. The second future scenario I would like to explore is to think about how this offering fits into a more unified and holistically thinking organization but still within the parameters of HR.

Workforce Analytics, Intelligence, Forecasting and Strategy (WAIFS)

Although the unified view and definition of Talent Intelligence that we discussed in Chapter 1 is far more robust, I would argue that with so much growth and development in HR Analytics, Workforce Planning, Talent Analytics and Talent Intelligence that potentially the future of Talent Intelligence could be a unified Workforce Intelligence function with subsets of Talent Intelligence, HR Analytics, Workforce Planning, Talent Forecasting and Planning, Competitor Intelligence, etc. all working under the banner of Workforce Analytics, Intelligence, Forecasting and Strategy (WAIFS).

What could this look like?

Within HR we have a range of teams and analytics offerings that are loosely aligned around the employee lifecycle for potential employee, candidate, employee, former employee with the contextual elements overlaid such as demand planning, external intelligence, cultural intelligence, etc. These would (loosely) align as follows:

- Potential employee
  o Sourcing Intelligence, Recruitment Marketing Analytics
- Candidate
  o Talent Acquisition Analytics

- Employee
  - o HR Analytics, Employee Engagement, Workforce Planning, Talent Forecasting, Talent Strategy
- Former employee (who then becomes a potential employee again)
  - o Exit interviews
- With some elements overlaying at all times dependant on need such as:
  - o Candidate Listening/Social Intelligence, Location Intelligence, Workforce Intelligence, Competitor Intelligence, Cultural Intelligence

These could all be combined to form a holistic Workforce Analytics, Intelligence, Forecasting and Strategy (WAIFS) function that not only looks at the current state and reflective state but also all forecast out and strategic decisions using both internal and external data sets. This would give leaders, our customers, the most complete and robust labour feasibility to date.

I would see this splitting into the following main pillars:

- Workforce Data Acquisition and Engineering
- Workforce Reporting and Analytics
- Workforce Products
- Workforce Strategic Intelligence
- Workforce Intelligence Decision Support
- Workforce Intelligence Futurists

Let's dive into these in a little more detail.

WORKFORCE DATA ACQUISITION AND ENGINEERING

As the name would suggest, this function is focused on 'acquiring data' before creating stable and scalable platforms and ecosystems for that data. This data could equally be looking at alternative data sources internally as well as externally. WDAE would be an interesting hybrid function, both looking at primary and secondary data acquisition combining the technical and non-technical. Within this I could foresee Candidate Listening/Social Intelligence, Exit Interview analysis and all scaled intelligence gathering, whether that is through web scraping, vendor relationships and API feeds or mass Talent Acquisition intelligence monitoring, etc. They will work with Analysts, Programme Managers and other Data Engineers across teams to understand the workforce management ecosystem, identify corresponding data needs and influence these partners on opportunities for collaboration and alignment.

I would also see the WDAE having a strong Workforce Intelligence Skunk works element. Originally the name given to a secret R&D team at Lockheed Aircraft Group, Skunk Works is now a name for a usually small and innovative group outside the normal research and development channels within an organization that looks to drive rapid research or prototyping. Within a Talent/Workforce Intelligence team these can be hugely powerful to look at what is possible with the power of the labour market data available to us.

The WDAE pillar is there to create the platform, the foundations and put the correct data model in place to enable the Reporting and Analytics and Intelligence pillars to thrive. They will be experts in data acquisition, architecture and data warehouse management.

WORKFORCE REPORTING AND ANALYTICS

Reporting and Analytics often get overlooked for the more glamorous predictive analytics, machine learning and artificial intelligence but the reality is that the vast majority of HR and workforce data usage is still very much in the core reporting and analytics space. At present, there are a number of teams within the HR arena that look at reporting and analytics for their various customer groups. This could be Recruitment Marketing Analytics, Talent Acquisition Analytics, HR Analytics tying in Employee Engagement, Workforce Planning or Talent Forecasting and Demand Planning.

By centralizing into one team, you can keep the customer focus by ring-fencing (if needed) but you will gain on three main fronts: first, increased economies of scale and efficiency; secondly, an increase in career pathing and specialization options (allowing for reduced attrition, increased employee engagement, etc.); and finally an opportunity to look at data sets in a more holistic manner that is unlikely to be looked at in siloed analytics teams.

How does employee engagement affect talent acquisition channel conversion metrics? How does external candidate or employee sentiment affect recruitment marketing spend? How has increased time to hire affected business performance or attrition? How are we combining talent forecasting, demand planning, recruitment capacity planning and channel conversion metrics to see the feasibility of hitting the forecast plans?

WORKFORCE PRODUCTS

Workforce Products would be a team of Product Managers that act as the intersection of customer demand and technical delivery. They would own scaled products such as self-service tooling, Data as a Service, Always on Intelligence, HR Analytics product suites, etc. They are responsible for the full lifecycle of these offerings and products from requirements gathering, data feasibility, build, user experience, product rollout, implementation, go-to market strategy and embedding, through to ongoing success and future product iterations and functional developments.

This role and/or capability is absolutely vital in ensuring the products and tooling built out are fit for purpose, address the business needs, align to the strategic goals and, most importantly, land at launch and continue to be successful post launch.

WORKFORCE STRATEGIC INTELLIGENCE

Strategic Workforce Planning and Talent Intelligence are in my mind often the ying and the yang to each other. SWP by design is looking at the organization's strategic goals and looking to establish a strategy with a mix of talent, technology and various employment models (buy, build, borrow, for example) to achieve these. Within this understanding, the external lens is absolutely critical. What is happening with the skill set in the market? How are competitors positioning themselves and how will this impact? What are the locations we are looking to build into and how feasible is that? What is our early careers programme and are universities creating the skilled individuals we need to achieve this? What is the Talent Gap SWP foreseen and how do we mitigate this using talent intelligence? These feel a lot like talent intelligence questions, I think.

I foresee that this could be merged into a Strategic Workforce Intelligence role combining both roles into one strategic workforce adviser that is fuelled by inputs from Workforce Intelligence Futurists and the Workforce Data Engineering function. This role would be looking at the three- to five-year strategic plans and at the feasibility and the potential risks. They would be senior strategic trusted advisers fully embedded in their leadership team's long-term planning.

WORKFORCE INTELLIGENCE DECISION SUPPORT

This is the pillar that I foresee to take on a number of the traditional Talent Intelligence offerings that we currently see such as: Location Intelligence,

Competitor Intelligence or Cultural Intelligence. This pillar is focused on one-off decision point support, likely focused on the 3–18-month timeframe. It would not be driving the long-term strategic thinking but rather the decision points that are already set in the longer-term strategy but where the situation has changed and you may need to reassess and reset feasibility or de-risk the situation. This would also tie in things such as Competitor Intelligence or Cultural Intelligence that can directly tie into product offerings such as M&A Intelligence, where a specific intelligence requirement is needed around this decision point.

I would foresee that where you notice a repeated need, or a demand that needs to be scaled (for example Always on Intelligence, repeated location analyses, etc.) then you would look for the R&A to build solutions that are owned by the Product team.

WORKFORCE INTELLIGENCE FUTURISTS

The futurist function is looking ahead and around corners for potential headwinds and scenarios that could derail the long-term planning. They will likely come from a background of labour, applied or behavioural economics or business analytics and, as discussed in Chapter 11 in the Talent Intelligence Futurist role, they will systematically explore predictions and possibilities about the future of the labour market and how it will emerge from the present. They would feed into Strategic Workforce Intelligence, looking at the feasibility of buy versus build versus borrow strategies and the long-term stability.

How will the changing demographics affect our workforce? How will automation affect the strategy? How will changing political situations affect the labour market movements and your firm's access to talent? How will a changing culture effect access to talent (e.g. increased appetite for gig working, self-employment or remote work)? How is the labour force participation rate affecting our ability to scale?

These individuals will also work very closely with your organization's leadership and internal economists to be the conduit and work at the intersection of macroeconomics and microeconomics.

This WAIFS function would then engage with and partner with a broader intelligence community, be it M&A Strategy, Marketing Intelligence, Organizational Design and effectiveness, Compensation and Benefits, Real Estate Intelligence or Competitive Intelligence, to look at data synergies. For example:

- Real Estate Intelligence would look at Market trends, Portfolio Benchmarking, Market risk but would also be interested in Location Intelligence.

- M&A Strategy would be interested in Synergy Evaluation, Target Evaluation but could also be interested in Competitor Intelligence, Organizational Mapping, Compensation benchmarking, DEI Intelligence.

- Marketing Intelligence would naturally look at product, market and customer insights and intelligence, but could also be interested in competitor intelligence and talent flows.

Talent Intelligence Centre of Excellence (TICoE)

My final model to think about is a straight-line evolution of today's current evolutionary path: a Talent Intelligence function that carves itself away from its current hosted function and becomes a standalone Centre of Excellence in its own right. This could be a centralized fat Talent Intelligence Centre of Excellence doing full strategic leadership, best practice and delivery or a thin CoE where you provide the strategic leadership and best practice and have the delivery mechanisms embedded within the business locally.

The reason I could see this evolving is the conflict around our natural home – whether it is in Talent Acquisition, Marketing Intelligence, HR Analytics, Workforce Planning, Strategy… the list is endless and the arguments ongoing. One of the main reasons for this is that Talent Intelligence is such a broad-ranging and holistic function and offering that it impacts each and every area of all organizations.

For many years we have heard about the evolutionary merging of Talent Acquisition, Management and Development into a total talent organization, but although we have seen some teams reporting into the same leader, any kind of synergistic or symbiotic relationship is largely yet to happen. I would argue that the reason for this is that is that fundamentally the functions are still working to very different KPIs, goals, visions and timeframes and, as we discussed earlier, these will all drive the behaviours and mechanisms within a team. This friction means it is proving increasingly difficult to truly merge these organizations. It is for the same reason that I can see Talent Intelligence carving out its own niche. The nature of Talent Intelligence as a function is highly variable from direct targeted decision support, rapid deep dive sourcing intelligence, highly strategic and consultative workforce or strategy feasibility planning. It is this ability to shift business rhythms and to be able to deliver true commercial impact with direct line of sight to both the top and bottom line of an organization that sets the function apart.

How could this work though? I would foresee a Talent Intelligence function that runs in parallel to current talent functions, be it management, acquisition or development. In the same way, a business stakeholder would have an appropriate partner from each of those disciplines at a given level, often with an HR Business Partner as a conduit. I would see them having the same relationship with Talent Intelligence. For example, you may have Operational Talent Intelligence Partners and Strategic Talent Intelligence Advisers/Trusted Advisers.

OPERATIONAL TALENT INTELLIGENCE PARTNERS
This role would mean working with Hiring Managers at local level benchmarking, decision support, feasibility planning, organizational design benchmarking, competitor analysis and salary benchmarking to allow for very customer-focused, flexible and fluid operational and tactical talent intelligence to affect decision-making.

STRATEGIC TALENT INTELLIGENCE ADVISERS/TRUSTED ADVISERS
Working with senior leaders on their future strategy feasibility, their work focuses on efforts that solve significantly complex or endemic problems. They are trusted to operate with complete independence and are often assigned to focus on areas where the strategy has not yet been defined. They will influence organizational priorities, business process and also business strategic direction.

Both these roles will draw upon the skills and services that run across accounts and business lanes, such as centralized delivery support, analytics, data engineering, product, etc. as discussed in the WAIFS model, but in this instance only within Talent Intelligence.

One thing that I would see as a large shift from the current state, albeit not from the desired state as highlighted in the 2021 Talent Intelligence Collective Benchmarking Survey, would be to look to move this Talent Intelligence function outside of HR. This is a big change from the other 'talent' functions which all currently sit within the HR organization. I would see this function reporting directly into the C Suite be it into a Chief Operating Officer, Chief Commercial Officer, Chief Financial Officer or Chief Strategy Officer, depending upon your own organization's decision-making mechanisms. The reasons I would position us outside of HR are the following.

- Building the external focus, and business credibility, needed to drive a future-proofed Talent Intelligence function is very hard while sitting in HR, which is often seen as an internally-focused function that is fundamentally a business overhead.

- In a similar vein, building out the commercial focus and growth mindset is very hard within a larger HR organization that is very unlikely to have business growth goals within and of their KPIs, goals, metrics, vision, etc.

- Similarly, HR have, rightly so, a naturally risk-averse and risk-avoidance culture. This is absolutely appropriate for the HR organization, but will limit and stifle innovation in a highly competitive talent intelligence landscape. Being carved away, Talent Intelligence teams can experiment more and build out Talent Intelligence Skunkworks teams to really push the experimentation and data exploration.

- One factor that has meant business functions often stand up their own parallel offerings is the flexibility, reactivity and speed that they need teams to work at in commercially focused, time-sensitive and business-critical activities. By design, many HR processes are not time sensitive, and pace is not the core focus, they are often cyclical and periodic with very clear and definitive deliverables and outcomes. This causes a fundamental culture clash with the time-sensitive nature the business demands from modern talent intelligence.

- One of the core aspects of any HR function is that it is formed with equality in mind and that is absolutely essential. However, with a Talent Intelligence lens, your customers and stakeholders absolutely will not be equal in terms of their impact or importance and you need to be in an environment that welcomes and in fact drives ruthless prioritization as your capacity will never meet your demand.

- Finally, repositioning Talent Intelligence will highlight to the business the power of labour market data. People are often cited as leaders' greatest assets and access to talent the biggest risk for leaders' strategies, yet they have the right talent data at decision and strategy points a worryingly small amount of the time. Seeing a talent analytics and intelligence team that is aligned with their business and ringfenced to their needs will help inspire confidence in the maturity and credibility of the human capital intelligence that can be provided to business leaders.

Summary

What an exciting future we have ahead of us. This is the moment to be the creators of our own destiny. Whether the industry trends towards a centralized intelligence function, WAIFS, a pure Talent Intelligence Centre of Excellence or something else is up to us. There are many opportunities ahead and the synergies, partnerships and development opportunities are limited only by our imagination and desire. Throughout, we need to be clear about who the customer is, what we are trying to achieve, then work backwards to create the model that will best deliver that. Whichever the model, we need to show the value and impact to the organization to ensure we are sufficiently funded to grow and develop in the most appropriate model.

From a vendor and technology landscape, I think we will see a huge amount of evolution and development in the next wave of product design as the landscape evolves, flows, merges and new opportunities open up as vendors cross-collaborate and cross-fertilize data sets and platforms.

TOBY'S TAKEAWAYS

- Develop the model best for your organization but think big and look to future proof your design.
- There are many opportunities to align skills and organizational/functional goals to create new mechanisms and organizations for Talent Intelligence to be a part of and to challenge the status quo.
- The industry is in its second wave and is developing fast. Use this time to co-create with vendors and partners to help guide and co-design the future vendor landscape.

17

Tales from the trenches

Throughout this book, I have always had the broader talent intelligence community in mind. It is a community I am passionate about and it has some amazing individuals within it. I wanted to ensure I had space in this book for them to share their voice and give some advice to those entering this field. With that in mind, I reached out to them and asked: if you could give any advice to someone starting out now, what would that be? If you started your Talent Intelligence career again, what would you do differently? This is what they said.

Kaylee Baldassin, Research Associate, AWS Executive Recruiting

Kaylee is a researcher in the AWS Exec Recruiting organization, focusing on building out market intelligence capabilities for the executive talent landscape. Before that, she was researcher for a boutique executive search firm, Caldwell Partners, where she partnered with VC firms and their portfolio companies to do executive level hiring. Prior to joining Caldwell, she led the secondary research function for the Venture Capital dataset at PitchBook data.

How long have you been in Talent Intelligence?

For four years.

If you could give any advice to someone starting out now, what would that be?

Think big about how to bring data into the recruiting processes. Always question current processes; there is always a better way.

If you started your Talent Intelligence career again, what would you do differently?

Build more foundational skills in data analysis.

How do you think talent intelligence will evolve in the next few years?

I think we will see a shift towards automation and more reliance on the 'intelligence' side of recruiting. Similar to what occurred with BI shifting, how businesses address internal business needs, I predict there to be a larger influx of this type of analysis in the talent market. There appears to be a shift between 'old school' ways of recruiting talent versus the new-school data-driven and automated ways. This shift will continue to progress over the next few years.

Arnab Mandal, Talent Intelligence and Workforce Planning professional

How long have you been in Talent Intelligence?

For 10+ years.

If you could give any advice to someone starting out now, what would that be?

Understand that no data might be correct.

If you started your Talent Intelligence career again, what would you do differently?

Enforce marrying external talent data to internal talent data.

How do you think talent intelligence will evolve in the next few years?

The current challenges due to high attrition driven by extraordinary demand for quality talent have highlighted that businesses need to focus more on talent to achieve business objectives. I feel that in the near future TI will be part of greater strategic decisions as companies start mapping talent intelligence to business growth.

Sam Fletcher, Head of Talent Intelligence, PayPal

Sam set up talent intelligence at PayPal and has a background in executive search, talent acquisition and consulting across the tech and financial services sectors.

How long have you been in Talent Intelligence?

For 5+ years in talent intelligence specific work alongside 10+ years in talent acquisition and executive search.

If you could give any advice to someone starting out now, what would that be?

Look for opportunities to build and gain experience in the foundational skills required in TI, even if these aren't gained in a TI setting. I'd outline these as being analytics and data science, data visualization, data storytelling, consulting skills, ideally some basic programming (Python or R), and a platform like PowerBI or Tableau. These skills will set you up for success in TI but can really benefit your career in most data-related fields.

If you started your Talent Intelligence career again, what would you do differently?

My TI career, like many, started in talent acquisition and executive search research, and my experience in TI was driven mostly by business or client demand. I'd take a focused approach on undertaking research and analysis to address big opportunities or challenges more proactively. I'd also have started scraping job adverts much earlier!

How do you think talent intelligence will evolve in the next few years?

With the increased focus from investors on talent-related data, and this data becoming more transparent, corporate talent intelligence groups will see closer partnerships with finance, audit and investor relations teams. We'll also see teams being built for private equity and venture capital firms and talent intelligence groups supporting corporate venture capital teams.

Rachel Engrissei, Market Intelligence Manager, Amazon

Rachel led a team of Market Intelligence recruiters who are part of Amazon's executive recruiting team for Design Leadership. They focus on hiring the most senior design leaders who will lead initiatives and shape the future of Amazon's offerings and experiences. The recruiting team is a centralized group that supports all products and initiatives globally within Amazon including product design, (UX/UI), brand and marketing design, user research, AI, ML, VUI, NUI and other specialties.

How long have you been in Talent Intelligence?

For three years.

If you could give any advice to someone starting out now, what would that be?

Be open to new things/learning.

How do you think talent intelligence will evolve in the next few years?

It will transform TA.

Soumalya Pyne, Talent Intelligence Analyst, Atlassian

Soumalya is an analyst who decided to indulge himself in Talent Intelligence some six years back. He has a demonstrated history of working across several business domains. Gartner TalentNeuron was his first stepping stone towards a successful career in market research. Providing strategic research outputs around the competitor intelligence, cost analysis, location profiling, etc. were his forte in Gartner. Currently in Atlassian, he partners with global TA teams and leadership teams to help and support strategic sourcing based on market research insights. Creating visually impactful dashboards, data interpretation and storytelling perfectly describes his job responsibility in a nutshell.

How long have you been in Talent Intelligence?

For seven years.

If you could give any advice to someone starting out now, what would that be?

Anyone who is not only passionate about data but also how that data can be put into plan of action can become successful in the domain. An inquisitive mind towards *why*, rather than *what*, can sail your way through the path of talent intelligence. You need to question the data at every point of your research to leverage meaningful insights that can help your organization build solid strategies in terms of hiring, business expansion, DEI, etc.

If you started your Talent Intelligence career again, what would you do differently?

From the very beginning of my talent intelligence career, I have worked across various domains like tech, automotive, aerospace and defence, oil and energy, etc. But if given a chance now I would like to start my career with a specific domain expertise establishing myself as an SME. In this case there are certain advantages, like knowing your domain entirely, latest updates within your area of expertise, better networking with SMEs with similar experience and intelligence on a majority of the employers in your domain.

How do you think talent intelligence will evolve in the next few years?

Talent intelligence has evolved exponentially in past five years. I believe it is a key area of interest for every other company these days. With rising competition among companies to hire the relevant talent for their respective positions, it is very important to gain some additional intelligence on how to stay ahead in the talent market. Moreover, talent intelligence is playing a key role in an organization to uplift their engagement rate, DEI effort, talent branding and strategic decisions. In my opinion, there would at least be one talent intelligence team in every tier one company (at least) in next few years and the tech companies would be in the driving seat in this case.

Evdokia Pappa, Research Associate and MI Analyst, AWS

Evdokia started in academic research by doing a PhD in the UK, but realized that this was quite isolated, before moving to commercial research in the market research field (agency-side and inhouse) and then to the exec recruiting sphere and got involved in Research and Market Intelligence. It was love at first sight!

How long have you been in Talent Intelligence?

For one year – four years previous experience in Market Research.

If you could give any advice to someone starting out now, what would that be?

Always try to see the bigger picture.

If you started your Talent Intelligence career again, what would you do differently?

Get connected with business leaders earlier.

How do you think talent intelligence will evolve in the next few years?

Big data, further automation, ability to drill to the detail faster.

Lee Yi Ting, Global Manager, Strategic Workforce Intelligence, Micron Technology

Yi Ting has been in the company and in talent acquisition for about eight years. She was presented the opportunity to start up the strategic workforce intelligence team around two years ago with herself as the only member and quickly expanded to a five-person team in less than one year as the customers and business saw the value of the work. They see the team to be a data and insights enabler to the greater TA team, working on analysing internal TA data with global talent market data and industry research to provide talent and market insights.

How long have you been in Talent Intelligence?

Around two years.

If you could give any advice to someone starting out now, what would that be?

Speak to your external network to understand more about this function as it is relatively new and many areas are still open to explore. Share your key priorities with stakeholders and get their inputs and any recommendations that they like to see. You might be surprised that they come with even better suggestions or creative ideas than you or others in the same role. Work on quick wins as you may have to justify the investment of the team creation. Do not limit yourself or the team to only specific areas of focus. Keep exploring and be open to ideas.

If you started your Talent Intelligence career again, what would you do differently?

A conscious effort to have regular check in with customers/stakeholders and request feedback in regular cadence.

How do you think talent intelligence will evolve in the next few years?

So many possibilities! I'm thinking it could be something like a Talent Strategic Function that models company current standing with market insights and best practices to determine all talent-related strategies.

Kim Bryan, Head of Global Insights and Intelligence, AMS

A seasoned HR professional, with a background across multiple industries and sectors, Kim specializes in talent acquisition and RPO and is heavily involved with the inception of talent intelligence and insights.

How long have you been in Talent Intelligence?

For six years.

If you could give any advice to someone starting out now, what would that be?

My advice would be threefold. Firstly, stay humble – remember that no matter how much research you undertake, there's always more to learn. This will help you to stay open to new ideas and concepts and ask for input at each stage. Which leads nicely to my second point: build in creative space to your day. Leave yourself time to think and analyse your work. That space will allow you to consider new and improved ways to present your insights and recommendations that keep the attention of your stakeholders. And finally, watch out for the rabbit holes! We love to learn and often a topic can be so very interesting that we find ourselves going a little off-piste (researching pharmaceutical manufacturing competitors and, four hours later, reading an obscure article on robotic vaccine therapies – true story!). Structure your research time and know when you have enough to make your piece meaningful.

If you started your Talent Intelligence career again, what would you do differently?

Be clearer on boundaries and limitations. In TI we love to problem solve, but that can often lead to scope creep or unrealistic expectations around timescales and delivery. Be brave and honest in negotiating what is achievable and relevant.

How do you think talent intelligence will evolve in the next few years?

Talent intelligence is currently constantly evolving and will continue to do so. We will start making real inroads into predictive analytics and harness more of the data that currently sits across different areas of the business. The possibilities are incredibly exciting and endless! One thing that won't change is the importance of our people – that ability to digest data and play back our findings and recommendations will remain at the core of what makes Talent Intelligence so beneficial.

Molly Starkey, Senior Market Researcher, Amazon

Molly has worked at Amazon for six years. She has spent the majority of her career in recruiting, but just shifted focus to be more research/talent intel heavy about a year ago. She is based in Minnesota.

How long have you been in Talent Intelligence?

Under one year.

If you could give any advice to someone starting out now, what would that be?

I still feel like I'm new and starting out. But I guess what has helped me along my journey is not being afraid to ask for help or collaborate. Chances are other people have similar ideas and projects can be more powerful with combined forces.

If you started your Talent Intelligence career again, what would you do differently?

Take more formal training in analytics/data.

How do you think talent intelligence will evolve in the next few years?

I hope that this role/function becomes more formalized in companies, especially larger organizations.

Sean Armstrong, Tactician, Pier C Navigation

Sean is a journalist, consultant and mentor with 30+ years studying leadership, motivation and talent.

How long have you been in Talent Intelligence?

For 30+ years, but the field has been tagged with many names.

If you could give any advice to someone starting out now, what would that be?

Listen, think, be true to yourself and ignore the naysayers.

If you started your Talent Intelligence career again, what would you do differently?

I would have avoided mind-numbing substances and been a better example as a leader.

How do you think talent intelligence will evolve in the next few years?

As with all booms, the dust will settle and simple solutions will emerge.

Jennifer de Maria, Shopify

Jennifer's background is in the non-profit sector and retail banking. She is an Agency Senior Hire Sourcer and Recruiter.

How long have you been in Talent Intelligence?

For two years.

If you could give any advice to someone starting out now, what would that be?

Network and align with leadership to show TI impact on business challenges.

If you started your Talent Intelligence career again, what would you do differently?

Develop more technical skills.

How do you think talent intelligence will evolve in the next few years?

TI leadership will be a sparring partner to CHRO. There will be a C-suite seat for the function.

Aliza Goldstein, Principal Program Manager, Amazon

An immigration nerd by trade, Aliza was always intrigued with global talent flows based on skilled, environmental, economic and political migration trends. With a background in international affairs, and a passion for high skilled labour, talent intelligence became a natural path to help multinational employers make strategic and informed global expansion decisions.

How long have you been in Talent Intelligence?

Eighteen years and counting.

If you could give any advice to someone starting out now, what would that be?

Trust the data, but don't forget to collect real-world anecdotes to tell the story along with it. Sometimes the data isn't giving you the full picture and you need to do a deeper dive to understand what may be going on. Don't be afraid to investigate and ask questions. These insights will enable you to elevate your research and delivery.

If you started your Talent Intelligence career again, what would you do differently?

If I started over, I would look to hone my analytical acumen earlier in my career. It is a very valuable skill to have when aggregating and analysing large data sets and to formulate educated opinions. I have had to work hard to upskill in this space to deliver better products for my customers.

How do you think talent intelligence will evolve in the next few years?

I would like to see multiple product integration with a focus on future trends.

Jenni Lenz, Genevieve Consulting Group, LLC

Jenni has worked in Talent Intelligence and Market Insights as a Talent Acquisition Consultant via Genevieve@ Microsoft/GitHub since 2005. She has 25 years of overall HR and TA experience.

How long have you been in Talent Intelligence?

Since 2005.

If you could give any advice to someone starting out now, what would that be?

I believe if you want to work in Talent Intelligence, it will be helpful to have direct experience in Talent Acquisition working as a Sourcer/Recruiter. I feel it is beneficial to really learn and understand the roles of the business/client and industry you are supporting.

If you started your Talent Intelligence career again, what would you do differently?

Right now, I cannot think of where I could have done anything differently but I am always up for new suggestions and ideas!

How do you think talent intelligence will evolve in the next few years?

I love the way the TI role has evolved over time. I am proud to be in a position that is proven to add value year after year to the businesses we support. I believe the function of TI will be mainstream across vertical markets and industries.

Rishi Banerjee, VP of Strategy and Talent Acquisition Management, ZTEK Consulting Inc

Rishi has over 15 years in the industry as an executive recruiter, market/competitor/talent intelligence.

How long have you been in Talent Intelligence?

For 10+ years.

If you could give any advice to someone starting out now, what would that be?

Understand the talent market and learn to create talent personas.

If you started your Talent Intelligence career again, what would you do differently?

Master MS Excel.

How do you think talent intelligence will evolve in the next few years?

1 Firms will become more touchy about where and who they hire from.

2 Data visualization for Talent Analytics will become the new norm.

3 Hiring managers will become more aware supported by the right talent insights.

4 Open compensation information will become an accepted norm and we will see different roles tied to a specific compensation bracket broken down by location.

5 Non-cash compensation (equity, benefits, etc.) will play a major role in defining next-gen talent intelligence.

6 Newer platforms supporting TI will evolve with a built in AI/ML engine to support scenario-based challenges.

Kim Haemmerle, Talent Intelligence Lead, Intuit

Kim has spent nearly 15 years in talent acquisition with the majority of those years in talent research. With a background in recruiting, sourcing, programme management and executive search, she understands the needs of businesses to proactively identify talent trends. Kim uses her formal education as a librarian mixed with her training as a head-hunter to bring strategic, client-focused solutions to her global work as a Talent Intelligence professional.

How long have you been in Talent Intelligence?

For nine years.

If you could give any advice to someone starting out now, what would that be?

Be curious. Always look for the question behind the question, because the root cause is never the first ask.

If you started your Talent Intelligence career again, what would you do differently?

I started my career in TI at a time where resources we take for granted today were either in their infancy (Talent Neuron) or did not exist (LinkedIn Talent Insights). And we certainly did not have a TI community! Anyone starting now should take advantage of the work done in the past decade and look for every opportunity to learn a new resource, methodology or platform.

How do you think talent intelligence will evolve in the next few years?

I think (and hope) Talent Intelligence and People Analytics will merge with Workforce Planning to become a one-stop human capital research hub. By bringing together disparate research entities, we can really start to tell FULL labour market and competitor stories, making exponentially larger impacts for an organization at scale.

Prashanth Kalyani, Head of Talent Intelligence, Hiringbot Software India Pvt Ltd

Prashanth Kalyani has around 20 years of experience in both BFSI and Talent Research domains. HiringBot is a sister entity of VipanyGroup, which is into staffing services. Prashanth is responsible for the Research Business including P&L, leading a team of researchers, Client Acquisition, Delivery, Innovations, training the team, etc. They run their TI business on the brand name 'Talent Chanakya'.

How long have you been in Talent Intelligence?

For seven years.

If you could give any advice to someone starting out now, what would that be?

My advice would be to focus on identifying various data sources and ways to collect the data and learn how they can make a story out of the collected information.

If you started your Talent Intelligence career again, what would you do differently?

Learn advance Data Analysis tools, understand what the clients or business team expect from me that will enable them to take critical business decisions. I would provide them with the insights and reports that covers 360-degree perspective.

How do you think talent intelligence will evolve in the next few years?

Considering the data as new oil and the digitalization in every industry and the rapid changes happening in the way business is run, it would be critical to understand the pulse of people and how they would adapt to the changes in the job market and what companies can do to make their employees retain or hire the best talent. There will be huge demand for people analytics. The AI featured talent tools will have limitations and TI will be effective only with human intervention; TI will witness multi-fold growth in the next few years.

18

Well that's a wrap

So, when we started out on this adventure we asked: how often are leaders making decisions based on gut feel with their brain on autopilot, all while we are missing the moonwalking bear through our organizations? What are those moonwalking bears? What are those blind spots in a business context and how can they be mitigated through effective labour market and talent intelligence? By this point, I hope you have a bit more of an idea about what those blind spots could be in your organization or at least the process you can implement to try to mitigate them.

The key point to remember is that this isn't as scary as it may feel: every journey starts with a first step. Look for data sets that you already have access to. Look at your HR systems, your finance systems and your recruitment systems. If you don't have the skills to interrogate the data, partner with those that do. This could be HR Analytics or it could be finance or marketing. It could be from your vendor supplier or it could be a stretch project for someone internally who wants to develop their data analysis capabilities. There will be people out there with the skills you need if you are open minded and clear about the challenge you are facing.

Throughout this, remember that data ethics need to be at the heart of what you do. Is the data you are using needed and are you handling it in an appropriate manner? Only use the very minimum needed to serve your purpose and always be clear about the purpose for which you are processing it.

Remember to look for those red flags. Start off by taking on projects and challenges that are within your comfort zone. Look for areas that look out of place, the outliers, where you can quickly build credibility with data sets you are comfortable with. Use these as the initial foundations to build upon.

Listen to your leaders and customers. They will give you buying signals as to what their pain points are, their fears, what keeps them up at night.

Think about how to address these best with effective talent intelligence. Be clear about how you define your customer and use this at the focal point to then reverse out, then set the mission, vision, goals and associated KPIs for yourself and the function. Make a clear line of sight between what you measure, what you set as goals, the overall direction you want to drive the function and how this aligns to broader business goals. This will help keep you going in the right direction in even the wildest of storms.

Know that there is no limit to the work you could get involved with. The product we offer is only limited by our own imaginations. The customer base can be broad and accordingly the type of talent intelligence, and associated product range, can be broad. Do not be limited by any traditional siloes or structures. Think big, broad and holistically.

Remember to try to align your Talent Intelligence function in the most appropriate place for you and your organization. There is no right or wrong answer. You need to think about what the key mechanisms and goals you want to align to are and who owns their setting and delivery that will allow you to align yourselves accordingly.

You do not need to immediately have all the answers and a complete offering; this is an evolution. At first you will feel torn, stretched in too many directions, a jack-of-all-trades but master of none and failing in all directions as you cannot do any one area as well as you would like to… but remember… 'a jack-of-all-trades is a master of none, but oftentimes better than a master of one'. Take this scrappy phase as an opportunity to experiment and play. Use this as a tactical advantage to move fast, have lots of initial pilots but do not commit to anything stable, structures, scaled or repeatable without having the support/capacity allocated accordingly.

Do not feel like you have to mature in a linear fashion. It is perfectly possible to fast track the evolution and maturity curve and create your own. The maturity model I've suggested is not a left to right, bad to good but rather an idea of the routes available and the areas you may see greatest return on investment and impact. You may well see different growth in your own organization the context will inform the direction and velocity of travel. Listen to the organization and react accordingly. Do not try to force fit any model into your organization if it isn't a natural fit otherwise you will surely see organ rejection and function failure.

You will not be short of tools and resources if you keep open minded. Be it paid for platforms, vendors, partners or suppliers, free external data sets, or internal data sources or internal partner teams. There is a plethora of data out there. Be creative, look to repurpose data sets from alternative sources and think about how data sets and partner team members complement each other.

Whether you are business, market, functionally aligned, centralized, decentralized or centralized and ringfenced is all dependant on your business and cultural context. Build a model that is most appropriate for you and the decision-making power base that your organization has. Be open and look to mirror existing teams and mechanisms where appropriate. There are pros and cons to most models, think about what benefits you want to drive and what sacrifices you are comfortable making to achieve them.

The skills needed within Talent Intelligence teams are broadening continuously. Embrace this. Look to build a function with a range of skills and backgrounds. Diversity in all its facets will be a huge benefit for your team. Look to actively and proactively develop this. Bring in interns, rotation programme individuals, work experience individuals, hire for skills, transferable skills, and potential rather than for existing job titles. This will pay you back multiple times over with the creativity and non-siloed thinking that your team will develop.

Think about how your team will develop. Be clear about career paths and be open and transparent about what is available and what isn't. Talent Intelligence is an incredibly competitive field that is growing rapidly, so being clear about what opportunities exist within your function will help keep people engaged and enthused. Equally, be transparent about when people are reaching the top of their growth potential within the team. Enable them to look at rotation programmes to give them broader skills. Look at how their career path will develop more holistically, even if it means they will move on to other teams or set up teams elsewhere. Your loyalty and transparency will be rewarded.

Remember that communication is key. Be comfortable singing your success from the rooftops. It is far too easy to be the unsung heroes in this function. Everyone will know the great work you have done for them but not realize the work and impact you've had across other teams. Be bold, communicate widely and openly with structured communications that clearly articulate your work, your pipeline and most importantly your impact to date.

Lastly remember there is no 'good'. All firms are driving their own functions in their own race in their own direction. Look to take learnings from others, and share your own hopefully, but know just because something was successful in another organization it doesn't guarantee success or vice versa with failure. Embrace the open Talent Intelligence communities such as the Talent Intelligence Collective; they are there for knowledge sharing. You are not on this journey alone. Many of us have faced similar challenges and frustrations. Know you have a community to support you.

INDEX

Note: Page numbers in *italics* refer to figures

CPSIA information can be obtained
at www.ICGtesting.com
Printed in the USA
JSHW061127151022
31726JS00008B/19